FRANK SAWYER
Man of the Riverside

FRANK SAWYER
Man of the Riverside

Frank Sawyer and Sidney Vines

Illustrations by George Woodford

London
GEORGE ALLEN & UNWIN
Boston   Sydney

George Allen & Unwin (Publishers) Ltd,
40 Museum Street, London WC1A 1LU, UK

George Allen & Unwin (Publishers) Ltd,
Park Lane, Hemel Hempstead, Herts HP2 4TE, UK

Allen & Unwin Inc.,
9 Winchester Terrace, Winchester, Mass 01890, USA

George Allen & Unwin Pty Ltd,
8 Napier Street, North Sydney, NSW 2060, Australia

First published in 1984

British Library Cataloguing in Publication Data

Sawyer, Frank
    Frank Sawyer.
1. Sawyer, Frank   2. Fishermen—England—
Biography
I. Title   II. Vines, Sidney
799.1′755   SH415.S2
ISBN 0-04-799023-6

Set in 11 on 12½ point Palatino by Computape (Pickering) Ltd
and printed in Great Britain by
Butler & Tanner Ltd, Frome and London

—— *Preface* ——

In February 1979 I was in a fishing tackle shop in Nelson, a small town in the South Island of New Zealand, looking at a tray of nymphs, some of which were marked 'Sawyer's Pheasant Tail'. 'Mrs Sawyer doesn't tie them like this,' I said. 'The tails are too long.'

'Mrs Sawyer?' said the owner. 'Frank Sawyer's wife?'

'Yes.'

'Do you know Frank Sawyer?'

'Yes.'

'Have you fished with him?'

'Yes.'

Turning to the shop he cried: 'Hey! There's a Pom here who's fished with Frank Sawyer.'

Some half-dozen fishermen converged on me and I was bombarded with questions. What was he like? How good was he? Some of them came back to our motel (my wife and I were on holiday) to see what a nymph actually tied by Mrs Sawyer was like.

I told them of his uncanny underwater vision, of his instant reflexes, of his casting, the rhythm and timing so perfect it was a joy to see, and how he could drop a nymph into a saucer at twenty yards. It was easy enough to tell them how good he was, but the other question – what he was like – I found more difficult. They knew of him from his book *Nymphs and the Trout*, from references to him in the books of other angling writers such as Charles Ritz and Howard Marshall, and from some of his BBC films which had been shown on New Zealand television.

I tried to explain that he was much more than a man who could catch fish and had devised a new way of nymph-fishing. He was a countryman who lived in a river valley, and all that lived in that valley was of abiding interest to him. He was walking in the snow one day with his old friend Brigadier Ernest

7

Oldrey when the Brigadier, pointing to some tracks, said, 'I see the fox has been this way.' 'No, not the fox,' said Sawyer, 'the vixen.'

All the creatures of the valley depended on the river, and Sawyer was a river keeper. It was the work for the river itself, described in Chapter 20 of Part Two of this book, that was closest to his heart. Then there was his work in inventing a humane vermin trap, mainly for rabbits, for which he was awarded a prize of £1,000 by the British Government – not noted for their generosity to inventors. This tale of toil and frustration is told in Chapter 22. As a result of his work, the law of England was changed and the steel-toothed gin trap, which he detested, was declared illegal.

He never gave up in his search for the truth. He observed, by eye and under the microscope, recorded, and analysed with dogged persistence. Slowly, inch by painful inch, by such men are the frontiers of knowledge extended. Such men are rare, and they usually have university degrees and research fellowships. Sawyer left school at thirteen and had a garden shed. And there was so much to say about the man himself – at times forbidding, prickly, dogmatic, but always transparently honest and (when he gave you his trust) the most rewarding of friends.

After they had left, I mused on how extraordinary it was that the fame of Frank Sawyer, the river keeper of Netheravon in Wiltshire, had reached across the world to the shores of the Pacific. If they were so interested here, perhaps others nearer home would be interested too. So the germ of the idea for this book was born. For I knew that my answer to their question asking what he was like had been inadequate. If this book should reach those fishermen in Nelson, the message is: 'Here is a considered attempt to tell you what he was like, told as far as possible in his own words. My role has been to fill in the gaps and to round it off, so as to make a coherent whole. I am sorry it has taken so long, but as you know, the Poms like to take their time.'

SIDNEY VINES
Salisbury, Wiltshire, England

Contents

Acknowledgements

Not the least of the pleasures of preparing this book has been in meeting and talking to those listed below who, without exception, when approached took the same attitude: 'Anything I can do for Frank Sawyer, I will gladly do.'

My grateful thanks for their time, for ransacking their memories, and for their company, go to: Peter Bale and Peter Maggs, both for many years with the BBC Bristol and producers of Frank Sawyer's radio and television programmes; Alex Behrendt of Two Lakes near Romsey, Hampshire; Alan Cook, who succeeded Frank Sawyer as head keeper on the upper Avon; E. L. (Jim) Davis and Lancelot Peart of Hungerford, both old friends; Anthony Hill of Twyford near Winchester who grew up with him; Douglas Newell of the Wessex Water Authority; Ernest Oldrey, who, as Chairman of the SDFFA*, worked closely with him for many years; Evelyn Prendergast of Bagber; David Rasch of Heale House, Middle Woodford; Wally Reed of Figheldean; Donald Scarfe, Secretary of the SDFFA; and Dermot Wilson, lately of The Mill, Nether Wallop. Mrs Margaret Sawyer, Frank Sawyer's widow, gave me access to all his papers, which she has lovingly preserved. Even more important, she has, in our many talks, opened her mind and her memory. She has been the centrepiece of the whole project. Others of the family who have helped have been his surviving brother Alf (who nearly drowned aged three – see Chapter 9), his sisters Molly and Anne, and his children Janette, Judy, Tim and Pat.

And in my own family I wish to thank my wife for tolerating my frequent fits of absent-mindedness during the gestation of this book.

---

*SDFFA and OFA

Sawyer was appointed in 1928 to be head keeper of the Officer's Fishing Association. In 1964 it changed its name to the Services' Dry Fly Fishing Association. OFA or SDFFA – it is the same thing. When Sawyer is writing before 1964, or about the period before 1964, he talks of the Officers' Fishing Association. I have used the name now in use throughout.

Extracts from *Nymphs and the Trout* are published by permission of A. & C. Black Ltd; from *A Fly-fisher's life* by Charles Ritz by permission of The Bodley Head; from *Reflections on a River* by Howard Marshall by permission of H. F. & G. Witherby Ltd; from *The River Keeper* by Richard Pease by permission of David & Charles.

The whole of Part One of the book, with the exception of my own introduction and some notes, is the work of Frank Sawyer and is published here for the first time apart from an extract which appeared in the Christmas 1982 number of *The Field*.

Most of Part Two is also by Frank Sawyer. In Chapter 12, 'A Meeting of Two Redheads' first appeared in the *Burnham-on-Sea Gazette*; 'Outwitting the Hunt' was among Sawyer's scripts for BBC talks, but the date of broadcast is unknown. Chapter 15 first appeared in *Trout and Salmon* (April 1968). Chapter 16 consists of three extracts from Sawyer's book *Keeper of the Stream* (A. & C. Black, 1952). Chapter 17 is from *Nymphs and the Trout* (A. & C. Black, 1970). In Chapter 18, 'The Netheravon Style' is from Charles Ritz's book *A Fly-fisher's Life* (Bodley Head, 1972); 'Nymphing in Stillwater' and 'A New Idea for the Buzzer' first appeared in *Trout and Salmon* (November 1961 and May 1970 respectively); and 'A Fisherman Observed' and 'Nymphing in Sweden' first appeared in *The Field* (June 1967 and September 1959 respectively). In Chapter 20, 'The Great Cleaning' first appeared in *The Field* (April 1957) and 'Chalk' consists of extracts from fourteen articles published in *Trout and Salmon* between April 1964 and October 1966. Chapter 21 first appeared in *The Field* (April 1951).

My contribution is the linking Chapters 13, 14, 19 and 22, and the summing-up in Chapter 23.

SV

PART ONE

Boyhood

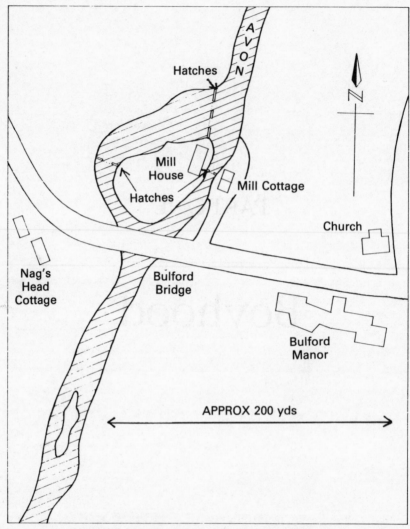

Bulford Mill Cottage and Neighbourhood
as it was about 1914

The Sawyers lived in the top half of the Mill Cottage. The bottom half was a store. The Mill House has been extended and new buildings have been built on the island on which it stands. The Ledger Hill family lived in Nag's Head Cottage. The narrow island below Bulford Bridge no longer exists.

The main stream flows between the Mill House and Mill Cottage, and it was through the narrow hatches there that Alfy was swept (see Chapter 9).

Introduction to Part One

These stories cover the years from 1914 to 1919 – the years of the First World War. Sawyer was aged eight at the beginning and thirteen at the end, when he left school and began his working life. These were hard times for villagers in Wiltshire particularly when most of the men, like Sawyer's father Willy, went to serve in the army in France.

It is almost impossible for people today to imagine what the standard of living was like. No running water, no electricity, earth privies the only sanitation, light from expensive candles or oil sparingly used. When it was dark, they went to bed. The living-room and kitchen were combined, and they bathed in a tin tub before the fire.

Just across the road on the other side of Bulford Bridge lived the Ledger Hill family, who figure frequently in these pages. At one time, they had owned 1,500 acres of Salisbury Plain and had lived at Bulford Manor. They, with a number of other landed families, sold their estates to the army at about the turn of the century, when the military first came to the plain.

Nag's Head Cottage was occupied by the Hills as a fishing-lodge. Mr Anthony Hill, who is still hale and hearty, was one of the boys with Sawyer in Chapter 3, and he remained a lifelong friend although the Hills left Bulford. There was a social gulf between the Hills and the Sawyers, but a common interest in fishing can bridge what appears an unbridgeable gap, and be a lasting bond. This is a theme which will recur in this book.

Despite the hardships, these tales of a vanished age are full of joy – the joy of growing up as a boy by the riverside.

1

Early Days at the Mill Cottage

IT IS QUITE POSSIBLE that one of the first sounds of the outside world which came to my ears just after I was born was the rush of water as it roared and cascaded through a set of hatches which controlled the river Avon by the old Mill Cottage at Bulford, in Wiltshire, which was my home. This being so, perhaps there is no cause to wonder why the river held such a fascination for me ever afterwards. Nearly seventy years have passed since the time of my birth, and millions, countless millions of gallons of water have passed through these same controls to travel on down the valley of the Avon, to reach the sea at Christchurch.

From the time I was old enough to toddle along its banks, I have been crazy about the river, and to it and to the valley in which it runs I owe much of the happiness I have had during my life. Memories of my boyhood days are very pleasant to recall. Some are a little hazy, it is true, but others remain as vivid in my mind as when the incidents occurred. Many fresh faces have come to the valley since the days of my earliest memories, and many old and loved ones have gone for ever. But still the stream runs on and beneath its surface are interests which can never fade.

Fish, fishing, and river and canal maintenance were very usual topics of conversation in our house. My father's father had been the miller at the old Bulford paper mill, which had been in working order up to a few years before I was born. The water of the Avon had provided the power to turn the machinery for this little industry, and in consequence the river and the controls had been of great importance. My father was born in the Mill House, which still stands just across the river from my own birthplace. He spent the early years of his life in very much the same way as I spent mine, and had a great love of the river. In later years, when he married my mother, they lived with my grandparents in the Mill Cottage, to which the old man had retired after the paper mill had been pulled down. My mother was born at Latton, in north Wiltshire, and her father was the canal keeper on the great network of canals which in my youth were still serviceable between Cricklade and Cirencester. As well as the canals, in this locality are the upper reaches of the Thames, and a small trout stream called the Churn.

Whenever a chance occurred I was at the riverside, or along one of the sidestreams connected to it. I was chased by the river keeper even as I have chased boys myself, but it was with a great difference. In those days I am quite sure I could run much faster, for there was a certain necessity to do so. If caught then, it meant a good thrashing with the nearest stick to hand, or with the old keeper's leather belt. Today we have to use words and threats of punishment. Perhaps, because of my own early life, I have been more tolerant to youngsters than some keepers I know. I think they all know my bark is far worse than my bite, and there are few who really become troublesome. Some, I feel sure, must have that same urge within them as I had, for to say the least a river can become a great temptation. I had many a trout and many a grayling, and I learned all the tricks of rivercraft. The young rascals tell the same tales today as I told when I was of the same age. 'We are only catching minnows, Mister' – and they fishing with a lump of bread as big as a walnut, or a worm the size of a young eel.

But what a thrill it was to have a big fish at the end of a line, with the fear of a breakage, while all the while having to have one's eyes alert in case the keeper was creeping up stealthily with his stick. It was the sport of catching fish that appealed to me. I was afraid to take home a trout. My father and his father had for many years helped with the preservation of the fishing. It was bad enough to get a hiding from the keeper. I did not risk getting a second by letting my parents know much of my activities. In my boyhood I learned much which I find useful even now. But times have altered considerably. The days of my grandfather, and indeed of my father, have gone, I hope never to return. Few indeed were the youngsters of that time, or indeed of my early days, who had a chance to see or to discover anything about water or aquatic creatures. Most had to be content with the scraps they overheard during the conversations of their parents.

A river, indeed any water, can provide a very fine subject for romance and, in those days of long ago, people had some queer ideas about natural history. The conversations of my parents interested me, but quite a lot of what they believed to be true I afterwards discovered to be wrong. People at that time had the habit of repeating what their parents had told them, and on various occasions I got into trouble for daring to argue about something when I knew I was right. For instance there were the mayflies. The Avon was always a good mayfly river and during their lives my grandfather and my father must have seen many thousands of them hatching from the river. Yet neither had taken the trouble to find out anything about them in their larval and nymphal stages. Both maintained that mayflies came from the caddis they could see crawling about the river bed. But I had dug out the nymphs from the gravel and the mud, and watched them hatch into flies. I also knew the kind of flies which come from the caddis. It is different today, of course. Boys and girls have every opportunity to learn about these things at school. In addition we have the radio and television, and the camera cannot lie.

19

The old river keeper of my boyhood days was a man I envied. His name was William Pratt. Though he was in charge of the fishing around my home at Bulford, he lived at Netheravon, as I do myself now. How grand, I thought, how wonderful to be able to wander for miles beside the river, with no one to chase him away! Whenever I had the chance to see him at work, I was there. He was then the keeper for the Officers' Fishing Association, whose stretch of the Avon extended for several miles, and where many of the officers stationed on Salisbury Plain came to fly-fish for trout and grayling. How I wished I could become a keeper too, and little did I think at that time that my ambition would one day materialise, and the greater part of my life would be spent in looking after the fishery he then guarded so zealously. This, however, is by the way. It is of my boyhood days that I wish to write, and of times which were very different from what they are now. To do this I must cut myself off completely from the present, be a boy once again, and recount just what happened then.

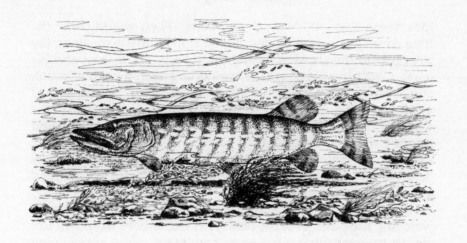

2

Snaring Big Pike with Father

THE AVON, like many other chalk streams and limestone streams in the south of England, always grew great crops of ranunculus and other types of water plants. Tending these to prevent flooding and to clear the reaches for fishing was one of the main tasks of the river keeper. The job of weed-cutting always fascinated me. Periodically old William Pratt and his gang of helpers would arrive in the garden of our house to start their programme of cutting weeds upstream to Netheravon, and I would watch their preparations. First they laid out a long length of lined scythe blades, and then they would don breast waders. Ropes were attached to each end of the scythes, and one man would wade across to take one end to the opposite bank, where another would be waiting to help. Usually there were four doing this job, two on each bank. Then would come the time when the scythe blades moved slowly upstream along the river bed to the steady and rhythmic pulls of old Pratt and his team. Great tresses of weeds would be sheared at their roots, and long round rushes would go bobbing up, stand almost vertical for a moment, like fishing rods, then slowly topple to the water, to be swept on down river with the current. I would stand in our garden to see the great rafts of cut weed being sucked through an open hatchway, then race around to the mill-pool below, and watch it being broken into fragments and swirled away downstream.

It was exciting. Sometimes as I followed along the bank watching the passage of the blades my excitement would mount almost to fever pitch, for a great bow wave might show going away upstream as a pike – a girt jack, as the men called it – was disturbed from his lie. Perhaps the great fish would show for a moment as he passed through an open space in the weedbeds, and I would listen to the comments of the old keeper. 'He were a big 'un you,' he would say. 'We'll 'ave 'ee when we drags.' By this I knew that shortly they intended to net the river, but to my shy question as to when this might happen there was only the same non-committal answer: 'Oh, thee wait an see. Might be two or three weeks yet.'

Until I knew for certain when the nets were to be used I was never satisfied, and would try and get this information from one or other of the helpers. The operation was called 'dragging' – a very apt word for it. The idea was to try to reduce the number of coarse fish and grayling, and at the same time to catch some of the pike. One net, called a stop net, was put across the river and a second one was taken some distance upstream and then dragged back downstream towards the stop net in the hope that all the fish would be trapped between the two. Usually the dragging programme coincided with our summer holidays from school, which began in late July or early August. Despite the crudeness of the operation, they did catch fish, and often large numbers, for at that time there were many thousands of fish of various kinds in the river. I well remember the waves and turmoil as big pike struck into the walls of netting to make the corks dance on the surface. I can picture the men getting in one another's way, as each tried to get a hold on a monster which, old Pratt said, was the one that got away last time, or he that struck out when we were weed-cutting.

It was at netting time that I learned the names of most of the fish which were in the Avon. By far the greater number which they caught were dace and roach, but there were also lots of grayling, pike and gudgeon. Occasionally there would be perch, and small bream. Sometimes eels would be entangled in the meshes, with a few big trout. For a while I was puzzled by the description of very big roach by the old keeper, who referred to them as 'billus boards'. Later I found this to mean that these fish, in size and shape, were like the wooden parts of a pair of fire bellows. Some indeed were big fish, for many weighed well over two pounds. All the fish, with the exception of the trout and a few big grayling, were pitched into heaps, the pike in one pile and the rest in another. The trout and the big grayling were returned to the water as quickly as possible. Then for a while pipes would be lit up and the whole gang would gather round to discuss the catch and gloat over the pike. When this ritual had been observed any boys who were present were given some fish to take home. Perhaps the catch at that one point would amount to two or three hundredweight, and that evening the smell of frying fish would be coming from many a cottage in the village.

Pike were very numerous in the Avon near my home at that time, and netting was the principal method of catching them. Dragging was seldom done more than once a year, and the operation never seemed to be as successful as it might have been. Still, this pleased me much more than it worried me. To be quite honest, I was quite happy when, to the dismayed shouts of the gang, a big pike would burst out from beneath the lead line or go over the cork line of the net to freedom and to his home in some deep pool. I then pictured myself catching that fish later on with a wire noose at the end of a long stick, when he was asleep or lying gorged behind some weedbed. Many times, as a very small boy, I had watched my father snaring pike, had seen him glide a noose of wire on his stick over the head of a pike, and the fish come hurtling out of the water as he pulled the noose tight and swung it out to land. In my young mind this was the only proper way to catch pike and, having an expert as a tutor, I soon got the right idea.

My father had been given permission to catch pike whenever

he had the opportunity to do so and, though this permit had not as yet been extended to me, nevertheless I felt it did give me an excuse to be along the river banks. I took very good care not to let the old keeper see me with a wire and stick, and if we did meet I would say I was trying to spot a pike for my father to catch when he was home from work at weekends. Still the old man was suspicious. I think he was a little jealous of my father and only wanted an excuse to put in a word with the fishing authorities to get his pike-catching activities curtailed. The chance for him to do this came one day after I had caught a pike of just over six pounds.

I was then about eight or nine years old and my caution had been forgotten in the excitement. When snaring this big pike I had been pulled headlong into the water. The fish had been lying almost out of the reach of my long stick, and I had leaned far out over the water to slide the noose over his head. I was about to pull and tighten the wire when the pike struck away towards midstream and so, instead of me pulling the pike, the fish pulled me. I lost my balance and in I went, though I managed to keep a tight hold on the stick. After quite a struggle I got the pike to land, and then scrambled out after it.

It was while running home, with the fish still dangling in the wire noose, that I was stopped by old Pratt. Apparently he had been trying to catch pike by laying a series of trimmers* with livebaits on them in some of the deep pools. On visiting them that morning, he had found one of them broken. Seeing me with the big pike made him to jump to the wrong conclusion, for straight away he accused me of stealing the fish from his trimmer, and demanded to know what I had done with the hooks and line.

Nothing I said did any good. The old man was convinced that I was not skilful enough, or indeed man enough, to snare a pike of over six pounds and land it. He took the fish from me and carried his tale to the fishery owners. They in turn spoke to my father, and he, in turn, demanded the truth from me. He tried

---

*A trimmer was a simple device for catching pike, in which a stake was driven into the bank at an angle of 45 degrees. One end of a line was tied to the stake and wound round it a number of times, while to the other end was attached a hook. This hook was put through the lip of a small fish. When the pike took the fish and swallowed the hook, he could pull line off the stake, which in a crude way 'played' him. Trimmers were also set to catch herons. The cruelty was barbaric, and Sawyer detested it.

and tried to get me to admit that I had taken the fish from the trimmer and in the end, thinking I was lying, he gave me a good hiding with his belt. I never forgave William Pratt for the trouble he caused over that fish. It was the biggest I had caught, and yet I was never to have the credit for doing it. To make matters even worse my father forbade me to go along the river banks except in his company. This was a punishment far more dreadful than any hiding but, as it happened, it was not to be of long duration. The episode over the trimmer caused me to hate the things for ever afterwards. In those days it was perfectly legal to use gorge-bait tackle of this kind, but it was crude and cruel, and I was pleased when the use of such things was banned by law.

That same summer there came a report of some big pike in a reach downstream from my home, where the fishing rights were owned by the Ledger Hill family. At that time the Hills were the owners of the Nag's Head Cottage, which is situated quite near to the Avon by Bulford Bridge. It was used as a kind of fishing-box by the Ledger Hills and one or another with their family would stay periodically during the fishing season. At one time my grandfather acted as the caretaker.

One of the daughters of the house had been over to my home to ask my father if he would go with her and her sister to try and catch one of the big pike they had seen. Knowing just how keen I was, Dad asked permission to take me, and to my great joy this was granted. We were to set off early on a Saturday afternoon. My father had hurried home from work, and I had waited impatiently while he had his dinner. It was a lovely day in early July, with the sun shining from a cloudless blue sky and with scarcely a breath of wind in the valley. The water was as clear as crystal and, as my father said as he met the two sisters, we could not have chosen a better time.

Dad dragged along a fifteen-foot withy stick he had cut the previous evening, and to the end of this was attached a strong wire noose. He and the two young ladies were soon busily chattering and at a respectful distance back I followed them down the river bank, proudly dragging along a second long stick with a wire noose already set, which was to act as a reserve. My knees were badly stung by nettles, as I was only wearing shorts and stockings, but this did not dampen my spirits. We were going piking, and the tingles from the nettle stings were not to be compared to the tingles of excitement that I felt. As I staggered along the uneven ground of the river bank my eyes were forever searching the water.

As a small boy I had acquired the art of looking through the water to the river bed, and I could see fish almost as well as my father, who was an acknowledged expert. About half-way down the first shallow, I spotted a jack of about three pounds lying within easy reach of the bank. My father and the two ladies had walked past this fish without noticing it, but my shouts soon brought them to my side. 'Oh, do catch him, Willy,' the younger of the two said at once. 'Yes, do get him,' added the other. 'What a clever boy you are, Frankie, to see it.'

My father turned with a smile. 'No, not I, Miss. Let the boy have a go. He saw the fish after we had passed it, and it is in a fairly easy place. If he frightens it out to midstream I can always wade out and try for him then. Have a go at him, Frank lad, and be as careful as you can.' Dad could never know the great pleasure he gave me with those words. The pike was lying perfectly still behind a big weedbed and, with my heart thumping like a sledge-hammer, I got my wire noose ready. Then, with all the caution I could muster, and with the eyes of the three grown-ups on me, I slid the stick with its wire noose gently out in the water, and well upstream of the head of the pike. With the drift given to it by the water, I guided the stick and snare down and over the head of the fish. How I thrilled as the wire passed behind the gills and then, with a strong pull, I tightened it, and swung the pike out to land.

I could see by the twinkle in my father's eyes that my effort had met with his approval, and, to the ladies, ('Chip of the old block, Willy'). He patted me on the shoulder and said: 'Well done, lad. That's a good start, Miss Ethel. He's got a good eye and a fair steady hand. I'm afraid I was too busy listening to you and to Miss Grace to be paying much attention to the river. But it shows you, doesn't it, you must have your eyes where the pike like to be. But come on, let's get down to the deep water, where you saw the fourteen-pounder. This light is not going to be better for seeing than it is now.'

The words 'fourteen-pounder' set my heart thumping again. I did not realise we were to try and catch one of that size. Why, it must be almost as big as the one they had painted and which hung on the wall in the Nag's Head Cottage. A fourteen-pounder! I knew I would not be given a chance to try for one of that size but, as it transpired, I did have my share of the fun. A few minutes of sharp walking brought us to the tail of the long pool where the big fish was said to be.

Dad had on an old pair of trousers and some old shoes. Taking his wire and stick he waded out to the middle of the river, which here was about sixty feet wide. Then, treading very gently through the weedbeds, he worked from side to side, and slowly upstream. 'Keep your eyes open, Frank,' he called to me, quite unnecessarily. Already my full attention was concentrated on the water just in front of where he was walking. 'He'll be at the top of the pool, I expect,' Dad went on, though how he knew this I did not know then. It is just knowing the habits of pike. Many times since I have made very similar statements. One just senses where the pike are lying. In its deepest part, the pool was about five feet deep. Dad went to one side of this, even though he was then up to his armpits in water. As he skirted the deep, so he poked and probed with the butt of his stick, but though I watched closely I saw nothing to excite me. Twenty yards farther upstream the bed shelved up gradually towards the tail of a shallow, and just there was a big bed of ranunculus. 'Now you watch the top part of the weeds, Frank. This is where he is, for certain.' Sure enough, as Dad waded slowly up through the long trailing fronds, a great pike came shooting out, making a big bow wave as he headed towards the shallow.

The wave stopped and I looked back, expecting to see my father hastening after it. But no. He was standing rigid, and very slowly rounding up his wire into a big noose. All the while his eyes were concentrated on a spot at the bottom, near the upstream end of one of the weedbeds. Slowly, very slowly, it seemed to me, he tilted up his stick and the noose went into the water. I peered closely at the short growths of ranunculus just a few feet ahead of my father. In a moment I had forgotten the pike which had gone upstream, for there, poking out, and clearly outlined on the bright gravel, was the head of the biggest pike I had ever seen. Quickly I turned to the two ladies.

'Stay still, you young fool, stay still,' my father shouted angrily. 'You stay still too,' he growled in an aside to the two young women, though how he knew they had moved I cannot say, as I was positive he had not shifted his view from the head of the pike.

Breathlessly I watched as the wire noose dipped down, and then moved nearer and nearer to that big head. Over the jaws it went, and on to the base of the pectoral fins. Then, as Dad pulled on the stick, the fun began. Twice he tried to lift the big fish clear of the water and throw it to land, but each time, as he got it to the surface, the stick bent, and it flopped back in again. What a flurry and scurry there was. Dad gasping, the fish splashing, and the ladies almost hysterical. In a third attempt to swing the pike out, the stick broke in half cleanly, and in trying to recover his balance Dad stumbled and fell. The pike, trailing the broken part of the stick, made a rush to the bank where I was standing. Without a thought I dived in headlong and grabbed the stick and held on grimly, while the monster pulled and plunged to get away.

I would have drowned rather than let go the stick, but Dad had quickly recovered. In a moment he had me by the collar with one hand, and grasped the stick near to the wire with the other. With a swing he flung the big pike to land, and then lifted me out too. Soon I was hearing the congratulations of the two ladies and, as I gasped to get the water out of my lungs, my father's voice cut in. 'Good lad, Frank my boy, good lad! He'd have got away for certain if you hadn't come in, but don't ever do such a daft thing again.' As to the pike getting away, of that I am very doubtful. The fish had been snared as only a master at the game can do it. The wire noose had been tightened just behind the gills and, as the big fish struggled, so the wire had slipped beneath the gill covers. It could only have escaped if the wire had broken. Had he gone off trailing the seven-foot length of stick, we would have had no difficulty in finding him, even in the deepest part of the pool.

To my young eyes, the head of the pike, as it showed on the gravel, looked as though it belonged to a fish of at least twenty pounds. But when we weighed it later it was twelve and a half pounds. I thought the first which had shown was the fourteen-pounder of which Miss Hill had spoken, as this too had seemed to be enormous. For the moment, and in the excitement, I had forgotten this fish. But my father remembered. Quickly he killed the big one, then slipped back into the water and took with him the reserve stick and wire. He knew, almost to a square yard, where that fish had stopped and knew too that it would still be there.

As he approached the position he tensed, then stopped, with his eyes fixed on a place near to the opposite bank. Immediately I knew he had spotted the pike, though it was much too far away for me to see it too. Slowly the stick went out, to drift downstream with the current. Then came the pull and all in one movement the pike was lifted clear of the water and swung out to dry land. This was no mean feat, as I found many times afterwards. That fish weighed just eight pounds, and to snare a pike of that size and weight while standing up to one's waist in water, and then swing it to the bank, is a job which needs perfect timing. Shortly afterwards he got a third fish of four pounds and with these three, and my smaller one, our sport for the afternoon came to an end.

Each of the pike, mine included, had been snared, as my father would say, under the gills. To catch them in this position, as I found out in later years, one has to make the pull to tighten the noose just before it can pass over the pectoral fins. The sudden tightening of the wire surprises the fish into making a kind of gasp, and then the gills open. As the gills open, so the wire noose slides beneath them. The advantage is that the fish cannot slip free, however much he struggles. With smaller ones, the position for tightening is not so important. These can be snared about mid-way along the body, at the point of balance, for one has little difficulty in lifting lightweights speedily and throwing them out.

Though thrilled, the ladies were a little disappointed that the big pike did not weigh as much as they had thought. However, many times since then I have discovered that there are various places in a river where the size of fish can be deceptive. This was one of them, and the pike appeared to be much larger than they were. In other parts it can be just the reverse, and big fish look to be much smaller. Much of the delusion is caused by the nature of the river bed, by light penetration, and indeed by the reflection of the river bottom in the scales of the fish. Fish on a sandy bottom always look to be much larger than those one sees on a bed of algae-covered gravel. Again, fish in very clear water always look to be larger than those in a murky spot.

29

The two Miss Hills were full of our adventures when we returned to the Nag's Head Cottage, where they were staying with their mother and other members of the family. I can well remember Dad and myself having our photographs taken in the garden with the four pike lying in a row between us. Many years afterwards I saw this snapshot and it was then very difficult to believe that the shy-looking, bedraggled and dirty little boy was me. It was an episode I shall never forget, and it was the start of another era in my early life. My snaring of the three-pounder had earned me the title of junior pike catcher, and to my joy I was given permission to go along the river banks whenever I wanted to.

3

Tickling Trout

ALL WENT WELL for a long time. Old William Pratt had forgotten the trimmer incident, or perhaps he had examined the inside of the fish for hook marks, which would have been very evident, and had then come to the conclusion that I had been telling the truth. One cannot extract a big triangle of hooks from the gullet of a pike without doing some severe damage. At all events, he no longer chased me off. I was happy with my freedom, but all too soon it was to come to a not entirely undeserved ending. One afternoon, during the summer holidays, I had two girl friends with me along the river. Please do not think by this that I was a girly boy. Far from it. To me girls were just girls – just a nuisance by the river, always falling into the water, screaming and frightening things I wanted to see or to catch. We were paddling on the big shallow just downstream from Bulford Bridge.

On the shallow was an island. I say was, because in later years this small island was removed in a general river cleaning and grading scheme by the Avon and Dorset River Authority. For many years, though, it remained there to remind me of my folly.

Everywhere about the big shallow were trout and grayling, all of which were quite easy to see in the clear sunlit water. We were all three quite happy paddling about and finding the various aquatic creatures in the weeds and beneath the stones, when one of the girls dared me to catch a trout. It is hard for a boy to be dared by a girl when he is young. At least it was for me, and that is the only excuse I can offer. As it happened, we were close to the island, and at the upstream end of it a withy tree was growing. Some of the roots of this tree entered the water and from them grew a thick fringe of pinky-coloured shoots, which reached down to the gravel like a kind of curtain. While we had been paddling, I had seen several trout go to cover beneath these shoots, and I had a very good idea where to find them.

'All right,' I said to the girls. 'You get on to the island and watch. I'll catch you a trout with my bare hands.' This was not said in any boastful manner, even though I was quite pleased to be able to show off. There was a small stream not far from my home, and many a trout I had taken from this with my hands from where they hid beneath the banks. I felt certain I could get one of those which were then hiding beneath the island tree. Egged on by the girls, I caught not just one but fourteen, which were of varying sizes up to one pound. It was just a game for me. The fish were tucked tightly in hollows beneath the curtain of withy roots, scared by our paddling. None of them had the slightest fear when they felt my fingers moving along their bodies to head and to tail. Each was grasped and taken to show to the delighted audience, and then it was put back into the water to swim away, and we would watch as it went out to midstream. But those silly girls could not keep still and quiet. Their excited yells and screams drew unwanted attention. I knew perfectly well I was doing something which could get me into trouble, and so it did.

The island was in full view of the Nag's Head Cottage and there, behind a screen of box bushes in the kitchen garden, a fisherman guest of the Hill family had been watching. A shout sent us all scampering away as fast as we could run, but I knew my trout-catching escapade would reach the ears of the owners. It did. My shock of red hair had marked me plainly as the poacher, and for a second time I was forbidden to go by the riverside.

The Avon runs through the garden of my home, and for a while I had to be content with the interests I could find under the eyes of my mother. Still, a little was better than nothing at all. I had an eel cage, a wire-mesh one, which had a hawk, or funnel entrance, at each end. It was oblong, about three feet in length, and a foot or so square. This eel cage was one of the joys of my young life, for in it I caught various river creatures as well as eels. Always there would be crayfish, and often bullheads and loaches. At that time there were hordes of crayfish in the Avon, and these would clamber into the trap, attracted by the bones and bits of meat and fish I put inside to entice the eels. I loved that cage.

To me it was a possession akin to a doll's pram for a girl or an expensive clockwork engine for a boy. Each day I would pull it out to see what was caught. Crayfish are very good to eat. Usually I would leave them in the trap until a half-dozen or more had been caught, and then my mother would boil them for our tea. They turn red when cooked and look very much like small boiled lobsters. With a pinch of salt, the flesh in the tail and claws is delicious.

Then one day old William Pratt and his gang came to start weed-cutting. I was hurrying to get ready for school and I had no chance to take the trap out of the river, as I had done on similar occasions in the past. As the scythe blades were pulled beneath the trailing weeds they fouled the cage. Up it came and, to my consternation, in it was a trout of about a pound. The old keeper growled out something to one of his companions and, while they checked in their pulling, he waded out and lifted up the trap. Quickly he opened the little door at the top and tipped out the trout. Then, taking the trap to the bank, he put it down and deliberately stamped it flat.

That old man could never know how near he came to breaking my heart, or so it seemed then. My cage, my trap for all kinds of river things, was ruined for ever, and never again would I have it to look at when coming home from school. I did not set it to catch trout, though it is true others had been caught from time to time. My mother always saw to it that these were turned free again without harm. Still, I suppose it was my own fault. Only a short time previously I had been caught taking trout from the river with my hands, and I suspect that this information had been passed on to the keeper with instructions to stop me doing anything in the river. I felt bitter against all fishing people.

◇　　◇　　◇

There were always shoals of big minnows – soldier minnies, as we called them – in our little length of the river, and I had some good fun catching some of these, either with a two-pound jam-jar tied to a length of string or by fishing for them with a bait. I liked fishing for them best, and had a rod made from a pliant withy, to which I tied a length of about a yard of cotton, with a bent pin at the end for a hook. I used tiny pieces of worm as bait and a plentiful supply of worms was always available. Minnows have big mouths for so small a fish, but even so a piece of worm about an eighth of an inch in length was plenty enough. This I would dangle on the hook amongst the shoal, where the largest ones could be seen, and then watch intently until one took the worm and the hook inside his mouth. Then, with a lift and a swing, out on to the bank he would come. Minnows are greedy little fish, and have not the slightest fear of a baited hook. With plenty of fish, and plenty of time at my disposal, I became very successful.

One day when I was occupied with my withy wand, without my knowledge old Mrs Ledger Hill stood and watched me. She had been over to pay a visit to my mother, as she always did when staying for a while at the Nag's Head Cottage. I say old Mrs Ledger Hill with no disrespect. To me she was old, and my parents always spoke of her as old Mrs Hill. She had sons who were married with children of their own, and she was also the mother of the two young ladies who went with us after the big pike. Indeed, it was a large family, and some of her grandchildren were about my own age. Two grandsons were staying at the cottage with the old lady just then.

Seeing me enjoying myself catching minnows gave the old lady an idea. This would be something which might amuse her two grandsons. The outcome was that she prevailed upon my mother to let me take out the boys and show them how I fished. Nothing could have suited me better. It would not take long to show these two how to catch minnows, and I would be in a different place from our garden. The following afternoon, as had been arranged, I knocked at the door of the cottage. The boys were ready and quite excited. First we went into the garden and cut some suitable withies from a tree in the hedgerow and, with some cotton and pins supplied by the housekeeper, we soon had our tackle ready. A few minutes with a garden fork in some boggy ground provided us with a good supply of small worms, and in a very short time we were all three busy at the riverside.

I had chosen a place just upstream of Bulford Bridge where it was shallow, and where there were thousands of minnows of all sizes. It was spawning time for them and here the great regiments moved about over the clean-washed gravel. Unlike many river fish, minnows will feed avidly while they are spawning, and this I knew. My two companions quickly learned the art of lifting the little fish and swinging them to land, and soon between us we caught a score or more. As we caught them, so they were returned to the water to rejoin their fellows in the ranks. The two boys enjoyed the sport as much as I did, probably much more, as I did not feel at all comfortable. My mother had insisted that I wore my best clothes and shoes as Mrs Hill had said I could stay and have tea. I had been dared to get my shoes or my clothes dirty. Foolish woman. She might have known it is not possible to go fishing without getting in some sort of mess, and that I couldn't really enjoy myself.

We tired of fishing after an hour or so; at least, my companions got a little bored and careless. So I took the two of them to my favourite sidestream to show them where to find and catch some bullheads, loaches, and perhaps some crayfish. But they were not satisfied. As I was pointing out the different hides a trout shot out from a weedbed and disappeared beneath the bank on which we were standing. Both had seen it and wanted me to catch it. They had heard all about my escapade on the island, but would not believe it possible to take trout with one's bare hands. For a while I refused, but after they said they would take all the blame if we were caught I said I would try.

The bank beneath which the trout lay concealed sloped gently down to the water. Until then I had been very careful with my clothes and shoes, but now I fear they were forgotten. Baring my arms and lying down at full length, I groped gently with my hands beneath the bank, and there I could feel the fish. Yes, I would show these two how to take a trout. It was as good as done. The soft feel of the side and belly of the fish sent the usual thrill through me. Without a thought for anything else, I eased forwards to get a good grip with both hands at head and tail and, as I did so, the bank collapsed under my weight. Before I could do a thing to save myself, in I rolled. Though the water was shallow it was deep enough to make me wet from head to foot. The trout slipped from my clutching hands and shot up the stream.

That ended our afternoon. Straight home I had to go; the promised tea at the cottage was to come another day. Still, the afternoon had been well spent. It is true I got a hiding for getting my best clothes wet and dirty, but soon there were other invitations to take the boys out. We spent many happy hours together.

That tumble into the water taught me a lesson. Sloping and unsafe banks must be avoided in future. However, it was but a few weeks later that I was up in the meadows about a mile from my home. Here the water had been shut off from the irrigation system, for at this time water-meadows were well maintained in the upper Avon valley. Usually old William Pratt, the keeper, would know when this was to happen and he would be along with his long-handled landing-net to rescue any trout which might have become trapped in the small runnels and carriers. One place he had missed and, in a small pool, with no hope of escape, were four trout each about a pound. At one side of the pool was a high bank, and here a tree root grew along in the water. It was hollow beneath the root, and the four fish chose it as a hiding-place the moment they saw me.

I had nothing to catch these fish with, and it was too deep to wade. I thought I might take them with my hands, but though I tried from several different positions the bank rose too steeply for me to reach beneath the root. It seemed certain that I would overbalance and tumble in, and my last ducking was still very fresh in my mind. If only there had been someone to hold my feet I could have managed. Thinking of this gave me an idea. As I came up the meadows a length of binder string had caught my eyes, and thinking this might be useful for something or other I had picked it up and it was in my pocket. There, at the right distance back was a sturdy bush and without more ado I tied the string around both my ankles and then, measuring the distance, tied the other end to the bush. Wriggling forwards and downwards until the string tightened on my feet, I lay head first over the bank, safe from falling in. It was easy to reach beneath the root.

In an instant I could feel the belly of the first fish and very quickly had it grasped at head and tail. But, try as I would, it was not possible to get back up the bank. I held the trout and tried to work up on my elbows, then finally dropped the fish back into the water and tried with my hands. It was impossible. I could not move. I became frightened, really frightened. For a long time I hung suspended by the string on my feet. My struggles only stretched the string and allowed my face to get nearer and nearer to the water. I became still more frightened, for I knew that if my face went beneath the water I would drown. Then, in panic and desperation, I began to shout for help.

It was fortunate for me that the old drowner who looked after the meadows was passing along a footpath nearby on his way home from work. He heard my yells, and quickly pulled me to level ground. As he saw the binder string on my feet, he demanded an explanation and then, in his deep Wiltshire voice, he growled: 'Why you dratted young vool, you mide a drownded yerself. This'll teach'ee to lave thay trouts to oul Wully Pratt in vuture, I'll warrant. You mist be vair mazed by thay vish. Wir did 'ee zay thay wir to? I've a mind to give 'ee a good larrupin', cos thee didst gee I a tarn, to zee thee danglin' ther' ead fust.'

I thanked him tearfully and begged him not to tell my parents. As I heard nothing afterwards I feel sure he kept his word not to.

4

Fly-Fishing, and the Pike that Bit

THOUGH NUMBERS of fly-fishermen came to fish the Avon in the reaches about my home, this kind of fishing had little appeal to me when I was a boy. These fishermen never seemed to catch anything, though they might spend hours casting flies. To me then fly-fishing was a dull kind of sport. I felt sure that if they had used a worm or a piece of bread they could have caught fish in the mill-pool, because many times I had done so without my parents knowing anything about it. When one evening a fisher-man began casting into this pool I stopped to watch, for at that time I had nothing better to occupy my time. I knew there were lots of big trout and grayling there, and felt sure he ought to catch one. As I watched, I became more interested than usual. It fascinated me to see the fly dropped without a splash at the far side of the pool, far beyond where I could throw a lump of bread with my withy stick. He saw me watching and to my surprise, instead of ordering me away as so many others had done in the past, he came to talk to me.

'Hello, young carrots,' he said to me. 'Were you hoping to see me catch a fish?'

'Yes, indeed, Sir,' I replied. 'That's a lovely rod you are using. What are you using for bait?'

He laughed. 'Bait, bait indeed. We don't call these baits! We use artificial flies. Look, here are some of them. Have a good look if you like.' Then he took a little metal box from his fishing-bag and opened it. This, like those we use at the present time, was one with various compartments in which were dozens of artificial flies of different colours and sizes. They were the first I had ever seen. 'There you are,' he went on. 'Now, which do you think the fish might take? You must have some ideas in that little red head of yours. Let me see. Aren't you the young rascal who tickled the trout over by the island? Come on now. You pick one out for me to try.'

Quickly I looked through the compartments and in one of them were half a dozen white-bodied flies with brown wings. 'Oh, these, Sir. I think you would get a fish with one of those.' I pulled one out to hand him.

He laughed as he took it. 'Why, that's a white moth. It's a fly I have used on the lakes in Ireland, just as it is getting dark. I've never given a thought to trying it here, especially one as big as that. So you think a fish will take it, do you? Well, I'll try it just to please you. But don't be disappointed if I can't catch one.'

I had suggested this fly because to me it looked very much like a piece of bread with a crust on it. I knew fish would take bread from the surface, because I often fed them with it. He tied it on to

39

the end of his cast, put something on it from a little bottle, which I later found out to be oil to make it float well, and then, with a few switches of his rod, he threw the fly to the centre of the pool. There for a moment it floated high on the water, and then down it went as a fish rose. One after another he took a dozen big fish from the pool on the same fly, and at the end of the evening he gave me sixpence and two big grayling to take in for my mother. He also made me promise not to tell any other fishermen that he had caught fish with this big white fly. Then, just as he was turning away to go, a thought must have struck him. 'You like fishing, don't you? Would you like two or three of my flies?'

'Oh, please, Sir. I would very much,' I replied, and my thoughts quickly flashed through my mind. Quickly he picked out three flies from his box and gave them to me. Not a brown and white one, it is true, but for the first time in my life I had become the owner of hooks which real fishermen used. Plans for these went speedily through my mind.

Though prized possessions, I was not to have the flies for long. I had found a little tin box to keep them in, and carried them wherever I went. The following Saturday I cut a long and whippy withy stick, about twice the length I normally used, and to this tied a length of about ten feet of cotton I had taken without permission from my mother's work basket. To the end of this, with some difficulty, I managed to thread on the fly and tie it securely. You might try some time to cast an artificial dry fly with a withy stick as a rod and a length of cotton for a line. Then perhaps you will realise why my initial efforts to become a dry-fly fisherman met with so little success. Somewhere in the garden, either in the potatoes or in the pea-sticks, I lost the first two of my flies without casting either out on to the water to the position of a rising fish. As I persevered in threading the cotton through the eye of the last one I felt sad. It's no good, I said to myself. You must have a real rod and line to cast flies and catch fish. Anyhow, I felt sure the flies were no good.

Upstream from our house was an old cattle bridge – the Black Bridge, we called it. It was a wooden structure for cattle to cross from one meadow to another on the opposite side of the river. It had guide-rails at either side, and the timbers of the footwalk were about four feet above the water. Beneath this bridge there were always some big trout, and many times I had leaned on the rail to watch them taking flies from the surface. One was a very big fellow of quite two pounds, which rose just near to the bank at the upstream edge of the bridge. Why hadn't I thought of him before? Carefully hooking my last fly to the butt of my stick, I trotted up the meadow to the bridge. Cautiously I peered over the upstream side and, sure enough, there was the big trout poised in the water. As I watched, he came up with a gentle glide and took a struggling fly. With hands all of a tremble, I got my fly free from the butt of the stick and then gently dangled it out over the water, thinking to let it drop and float to the fish. What happened caught me altogether by surprise. The trout saw the fly as it hung suspended a good foot from the water, and like a bullet he came quite clear of the surface to grab it in his mouth. As he snatched, so did I. I knew the hook caught in his mouth as for a moment I felt the rod bend, and then my cotton, minus the fly, went sailing up in the air. That was my first experience of fishing with an artificial fly. Sadly I made my way back home with the memory, a memory that has lasted until now. Even today as I write I can visualise that big fish as he came hurtling up, a thrill which can never fade.

◇　　◇　　◇

At school we had nature lessons – not the kind which take place in schools now, it is true, but nevertheless they always interested me. One afternoon we were to have a drawing lesson, and in the morning all those going home for their dinner were asked to bring a subject of their own choosing from nature. My choice was a pike. I knew a back stream where there were several, of about two pounds each. It was a nice clear day with no wind to ripple the water, and the moment our dinner was over I went with my wire and stick to try and get one. In a very short time I discovered a fish which was lying half asleep in a rush bed, and it became an easy victim. Out he came and I tapped him on the head with a short piece of stick to kill him. I took the pike home, wrapped it in a newspaper and took it to school.

On arrival there the pike caused a great sensation, as of course many of the pupils had never seen one, alive or dead. They all crowded round and for a time I was the centre of attraction. Our teacher hesitated before giving me permission to try to sketch it, but eventually she decided it would be something unusual, and,

41

as my desk companion had nothing himself, he could also make a drawing. Between us we propped the pike up so that it showed to the best advantage and, to the envy of all the boys and girls around, we got on with our sketching. Working carefully, I made a fair outline of the body and head. Penny, my companion, had been a little quicker, and was about to draw in some of the teeth. One tooth was partially covered with a piece of grass, so, pushing his finger forward, he tried to poke this off.

What happened then was much too quick for me to see. As Penny touched the tooth, the pike must have opened and closed his jaws with a snap. With a howl which startled the whole school, Penny shot up off his seat like a jack-in-the-box, with the fish dangling from his finger. With a jerk which tore two long gashes, he pulled his finger free, while the pike dropped to the floor and went jumping and slithering beneath the desks. With girls shrieking and boys laughing it came to rest beneath our teacher's desk, and there I bent to pick it up.

Often I wonder why there are so many people who act before thinking. Here was a case in point. As the cane slashed three times in quick succession across the tight seat of my shorts, I let out a yell which rivalled that of Penny. 'Take the brute outside immediately and kill it, you disgraceful boy. How dare you bring a live fish to school. Leave it in the lobby and then come back here.' So outside I took the pike and gave it a rap with the leg of a chair which would have killed a shark, and then back to the classroom. There, before white-faced girls and solemn boys, Penny was having his finger dressed with a clean white bandage. There, a few moments later, I had my fingers dressed too, but with the cane. Needless to say, we did not finish our drawings. It was a pity, too, as I had made an eye which looked almost lifelike.

5

An Idyll at Latton

SOMETIMES our summer holidays were spent at my mother's home in Latton, which is a little village north-west of Cricklade, in Wiltshire. This was always exciting, for my mother's father was the canal keeper on the network of canals which link up Berkshire, Wiltshire and Gloucestershire. Many miles of these canals were under his control. The public had certain rights of way along the towpaths, but he, being the keeper, gave us, his grandchildren, a right to do as we pleased, as long as it caused him no annoyance. It was a paradise for me for in addition to having the canals to wander along there was the trout stream called the Churn which travelled down through the meadows from the direction of Cirencester. A short distance away from this the upper reaches of the Thames meandered in a series of rushy shallows and muddy pools.

My grandfather's house stood beside a small lock, which was called the Basin. The house had been built expressly for the canal keeper and it was so sited that it commanded a view all around for a considerable distance. The lock was oblong, about eighty yards long and some thirty yards wide. Here, in years past, many of the barges which used the canals would pull in to spend the night. Nearby were walled-in paddocks where the tow horses were turned loose to graze. The lock was controlled by big gates at either end and usually the water in the deepest part was about four feet deep. In this big lock there were hundreds of fish and, being so close to the house, it was an ideal place for us all to fish while under the watchful eyes of our parents.

It was here I first used a real rod with the correct line and hooks for coarse fishing. My grandfather and my two uncles, his sons, were all keen fishermen, and finding that I was so interested they gave me every encouragement. I had to share the tackle with my brothers and my cousins, who were also on holiday there at the time, but they had made us up an outfit which gave us all a good chance to catch fish. The fish, though mostly small, were very numerous, and several different species were present. Included were fair numbers of perch and tench, which were two fish I saw little of in the Avon at home. We caught numbers of these small fish, indeed, I found them to be far less difficult than the minnows at home. But the larger ones defeated us. It was fascinating to try and get these bigger fish to take the bait and then hook them before they could spit it out again. Here I learned much about coarse fish in still waters.

We were forbidden to fish in the trout stream, or to go near to the Thames unless one of the grown-ups was with us. The Churn, though a tiny river compared with the Avon I knew, held some very big trout. There were stories of some which weighed over ten pounds, and though I never did see one of that size I did see one of seven. The little stream was packed with water snails and it was these, my grandfather told us, that formed the main food supply and allowed the fish to grow big. He was right, of course, as I found out for myself in later years. Trout do grow quickly in a water which produces an abundance of molluscs if they take them as food. In the Churn at that time there were many thousands, and a great variety.

River snails never live longer than a year or so and each summer it is possible to find hordes of empty shells. I remember one afternoon we collected as many different sizes and shapes of shell as we could find, and then threaded them all on to a length of twine to make necklaces for our two girl cousins. To my grandfather and my uncles they were all just snails – big ones and little ones, curly ones and flat ones, some soft, some hard. None of them knew the various species and families, and none had the slightest idea which was the favourite amongst them for trout. I know we threaded up more than twenty different-shaped shells and suspect, from what I know now, that the Churn held some of nearly every freshwater kind.

It was while we were staying at the Basin one summer that tragedy came to the little Churn. My recollections are of considerable excitement and bustle waking me up early in the morning and then, at breakfast, of hearing snatches of conversation amongst my grandparents and my aunts and uncles. Mother then told us that the trout stream had been poisoned and that all the fish in it were dying. This, unfortunately, was the truth. The little river runs along just at the end of the garden of the house and there, as we stood watching, we could see trout milling and struggling at the surface. Many were floating along belly up to the sky, with fins feebly moving. I was surprised to see the great numbers and the size of many of them, for though I had been near to this part many times, I only saw fish now and then. About the river, stationed at different parts along each side of the stream, were lots of strangers with nets on long handles. Buckets and baths were everywhere.

My grandfather and my two uncles were wading in the centre of the river, each with a net and a bucket. As the exhausted trout were lifted out they were taken in the buckets to a cart lodged with big barrels of clean water where someone was standing by to look after them. All trout which could be kept alive were to be transferred by the cart to another river nearby but, judging from the serious expression on the faces of my grandfather and others, and the great pile of dead trout which was on the bank, I fear there were few which survived.

Trout of up to seven pounds were taken from the Churn that day. Afterwards we learned that through carelessness or thoughtlessness someone had released some effluent at a milk factory some distance upstream. In a very short time this had swept downstream in bulk with the flow of water, to rob the river of oxygen and kill as it went. To this day the Churn has never produced the numbers of beautiful trout which were there before this pollution occurred, for not only were the fish destroyed but much of the food supply too. The last time I saw this part of the stream, a few years ago, it was but a muddy uncared-for ditch. Then there was only an occasional trout with a few coarse fish and pike in the deep pools. This was but one of many serious pollutions which occurred about that same period for at that time few people realised just how toxic certain discharges could be to aquatic life.

To me, as a boy, the incident aroused interest only for a short time. Tragic as it was, the full significance did not occur to me. Besides, from our sporting point of view we had lost nothing. The trout stream had always been out of bounds for us and there were plenty of fish in the canals. My grandfather had a boat. We called it a boat but really it was a cumbersome, flat-bottomed punt, which he used from time to time to carry spoil, timbers, etc., to repair weak places in the banks or towpaths along the canals. Still, it was watertight and in it we could have lots of fun. What I liked best of all was going along the deep parts of the canal and peering down to the weedy bottom to see the fish.

Sometimes, as we poled along, there would be a great surge and a swirl of water as a big pike was disturbed from where he had been basking in the sun near the surface. I was fascinated by the stripy perch as they weaved in and out amongst the weed-stems, and the great bream which really did look like the 'billus boards' of old Pratt and his helpers. Both were numerous in the canals. They, together with a great shoal of others – roach, dace and rudd – would go ahead of the boat until it seemed there were thousands from bank to bank. With the bright sun shining down on them, these vast shoals appeared to be more numerous than they were in reality. Each cast a shadow which of course moved with them. As we poled along, so the fish would move onwards too, and at times they might go ahead of us for as much as two or three hundred yards. Then suddenly, just as though an order had been given, the whole shoal, large and small alike, would turn, and back under the boat they would go.

In the house at the Basin were the skins of several big otters, and also some heads which had been preserved and mounted. My grandfather's brother was a very clever amateur taxidermist and had the secret of the successful dressing of skins and the stuffing and mounting of both animals and birds. Otters were quite common in this locality and it was not unusual to see one from the windows of the house as it hunted in the big lock or the trout stream. My grandfather received a guinea from the owner of the trout fishery for any he could kill, and he was also paid a bonus of half a crown for the heads of any herons he could shoot. There were plenty of herons about the Avon near my home at Bulford and of course I knew them well, and the damage they could do in a trout stream. In a case in the house was a stuffed bittern and this was the first I had ever seen. Bitterns were rare birds in that part, as they are in the upper Avon valley. This was one my grandfather had shot. He had been waiting for duck and it was almost dark when the bird flew within range. He shot, thinking it was a heron, for in flight there is some similarity, especially in semi-darkness. He was sorry afterwards as he thought it could have been one of a pair which might have stayed to nest in the locality.

All about Latton were marshes and rushy lands. It was an ideal place for wildfowl, and ducks of various kinds lived on the canals. There were also large numbers of moorhens and coots, and lots of dabchicks. Rushes and sedges fringed the edges of the canals in many places, and we would hunt these for nests and eggs. Coots were never very plentiful on the upper Avon and it was here that I discovered that their eggs were quite as good to eat as those of the moorhen. So we would take any which we knew were freshly laid. We never ate the eggs of the dabchick for some I once tried had tasted muddy and fishy.

When searching for eggs we would take with us a dessert spoon tied securely to the end of a long stick. Any nests which were out of reach by hand from the bank were robbed with the spoon and stick. It needs a steady hand to extract eggs with a spoon at the end of a long stick, and many a one was tilted out and lost for ever. A nest was never robbed of its clutch until the first egg had been tested. To test for freshness an egg would be held in the palm of the hand and then immersed in the water. If it remained perfectly level then there was every reason to think the bird had not started to sit, or brood. If the egg tilted off balance, with big end uppermost, we knew the chick had started to form. If it floated then we knew the eggs were very near to hatching time or were addled.

Though we often found ducks with their clutches of young ones we always left these severely alone. It would amuse us to see the ducklings dive and swim along underwater, and then a head appear here and another there to watch until we had gone. We were never tempted to chase the old duck when she went flapping away, feigning a broken wing to attract our attention. We knew all about this habit. My grandfather had the shooting rights and it was here at the Basin that I had my first taste of wild duck and wild goose. Wildfowl shooting then started on the first day of August. My grandmother was an excellent cook and I always enjoyed all of the waterbirds she prepared and cooked.

Parts of the Thames were very rushy. Bullrushes grew very sturdily in the water and from time to time I was allowed to go with one of my uncles to cut some, and lay them out to dry. At the house by the Basin they carried on a little industry in basket making and weaving rush mats. Most of the baskets made were for the farm workers in the locality to carry their food and drink in, and there was quite a demand for them. The rushes would be cut green with a small reaping hook and then laid out along the banks of the river in a thin layer. When thoroughly dry the round rushes could be flattened and they were very strong. I always enjoyed paddling about the shallows to cut bundles and carry them ashore. Often the stems were covered with the eggs of snails, which made them all slimy to the touch where they had been underwater. On them too would be a great variety of other life and I fear many creatures had to die when the rushes were laid out to dry.

It was, I think, the winter of 1917–18 when we had lots of hard frost. My aunt, living at the Basin, had written to my mother to say that the canals and the big lock were all frozen over, and that it was quite safe to skate. She asked my mother if she would care to bring along her family for a week or two and have some fun with other sisters and their children who had agreed to come. It was early January and for some reason – a bad epidemic of influenza, I believe – our school had been closed, as indeed had many others about the country. After thinking it over, mother decided we would go. My father was still in the army. So too were all my uncles, but two of these were home on leave.

When we arrived at the Basin it was easy to see that what my aunt had written was true. The big lock was one great sheet of ice, and all the canals were frozen over. It was possible to skate for miles. Though none of us youngsters could skate, or indeed had any ice skates, we enjoyed being able to go sliding and to watch others more fortunate who were equipped with skates and knew how to use them. Many people from the nearby towns of Cricklade and Swindon had their fun on the canals, but they were not allowed on the big lock. This was ours, and it was ideal for ice hockey. With the grown-ups and the children there were plenty to make up two sides. We had hockey sticks of all sizes and shapes, and this game amused us for hours.

Day after day the frost held. I had not given a thought to fishing until one morning an uncle brought in a great pike he had caught. Later that same day he brought in a second. From the scraps of conversation I was able to hear, I found out that he had caught these through a hole in the ice. To me, at that time, there was only one way to catch a pike and that was by snaring it. Next day I fashioned a wire and stick and out on to the ice of the lock I went. It was not easy to see through the ice owing to the scrapes, slashes and rashers, as we called them, made by our skating and sliding. However, behind one of the goals of our hockey pitch the ice was much less marked and I could see through it and into the clear water below. Crawling about, I could see numbers of small fish, and then I found a pike which was lying perfectly still on the bottom.

He took no notice as I moved about on the ice above him to get the best view. He was a fish of about two pounds. I had with me a spike which was a broken-off tine of a garden fork. Thinking about what my uncle had said, I set about digging a hole through the ice, every now and then peering down to see if the pike had moved. The hole was quite four inches in diameter. With the utmost care I dipped out the fragments of ice with my hand and then looked down on the back of the pike some three feet below. Every feature was plainly visible to me and with all the caution I could muster the wire noose was pushed through and then guided down.

The pike remained perfectly still while the noose was eased gently over his head and on to the front fins. Then, with a sharp upward pull I had him. Up he came, but once again I had forgotten something. I could not get him through the hole. However with the pike jammed tightly against the ice it was possible to enlarge the hole quickly with the spike. Soon he came through, with the wire noose cutting tightly into his gills.

Just as I got him through and on to the ice my grandfather appeared. Apparently he had been watching without my knowledge. How he laughed! Calling my uncles he told them the story. 'Well I never did,' he said, 'that's one up on you, Jim. What ever is the boy going to do next? Fancy wiring a pike through a hole in the ice. I would never have thought it possible.' The amusing thing, apparently, was that my uncle had caught his two fish with livebaits on hooks which he had lowered through a hole in a big pond where the water had not frozen over completely, a very different method of fishing from my own.

Being talked about and praised over this episode made me eager to try again. Next morning all the other children went off to the village. I did not want to go shopping. I much preferred to be alone and try for another pike. Soon I was out on the ice of the big lock, crawling about on my hands and knees and, after a diligent search, I was rewarded by spotting a fish of several pounds which was lying quite still in a bed of weeds. Like the smaller one on the previous day, he appeared to be quite unaware of my presence above him and, working as fast as I could, it was not long before I had dug a hole through the ice to the water. Obviously the fish sensed, or saw, some movement, for just as I was clearing the ice fragments he struck away towards the centre of the lock. With my face in cupped hands close to the ice, like a dog on a scent, I crawled in the direction he had gone and discovered him lying still again. With greater caution I dug a second hole but once more the fish moved before I could put my noose through. This same thing happened time after time, until a dozen or so holes had been dug all about the ice, and it was while I was digging yet another that the other children returned from their expedition to the village.

They had planned a hockey match for the afternoon. In my eagerness to get the big pike no thought of hockey, of time, or indeed of anything else, had entered my mind. The hockey pitch was ruined for holes were everywhere about it, with chips of ice looking very white on the dark background. My mother was very vexed and had it not been for intervention by my grandfather I feel sure I would have had a thrashing. 'Don't beat him,

Prue,' he said. 'I won't have you beat him. The little chap didn't think, that's all.' I was saved a hiding but all that afternoon I had plenty of time to think. While all the other children were out enjoying themselves sliding on the canal, I had to stay in our bedroom alone.

Still, it was worth any punishment. I have never forgotten the excitement I had in chasing that pike from place to place, and next day all was well again. A film of ice had quickly formed on the water in the holes and my grandfather then filled them up level with the rest of the ice, and swept away all the chips I had made. By morning the holes were frozen solid and it was safe to skate and slide. I had no chance to try for other pike and it was to be many years before I saw others beneath ice. This time it was on the upper Avon in 1934 but the ice on the river was not thick enough to bear my weight.

What interested me most about this episode was the fact that the pike, and indeed many other fish, were not scared as I crawled about the ice above them. Thinking it over afterwards, I came to the conclusion that the vision of the fish was limited to the surface of the water, and that it was not possible for them to see up through the ice as I could see downwards. I think, with the sky above, the ice formed a ceiling which was opaque. This let in a shaft of light immediately it was cut through and perhaps accounted for the reaction of the big pike in moving from suspected danger.

NOTE

The Sawyer Family

Frank Sawyer had a happy relationship with both his parents, especially his father, with whom he shared a love of the river and of fishing. His mother appears as something of a disciplinarian, but this was not really the case. His father was actually the stricter of the two, but for much of this period Willy Sawyer was away in the army in France. The whole burden of bringing up the family of six (three boys and three girls) fell to his mother. When she beat Frank for taking bread for bait, or for damaging his clothes, it was becasue she was at her wits' end to feed and clothe them.

Willy Sawyer was a quiet, kind, domesticated man. Everyone liked him, but he was not forceful, and did not make much impression outside his family. He used to cook the Sunday breakfast and take it up to the family in bed. He liked to be immaculate in his dress, and would rather go without breakfast than go out with dirty boots. After Frank married in 1935 and went to live in Netheravon, Willy would cycle the five miles there every Sunday morning, stay ten minutes, and pedal slowly but steadily back, stopping at the local for a lunch-time drink – a man of regular habits. He died in 1950.

Prudence Sawyer, Frank's mother, was the driving force, and Willy was content to let her be. There is a photograph of her, aged twenty-six, a young married woman in the high fashion of 1903 – a long-skirted costume with a tiny waist and a wide-brimmed hat decorated with flowers. She looks pretty and healthy, but what is striking is the confident and determined way she faces the camera. This will-power Frank seems to have inherited. She was an accomplished needlewoman, she could play the mandolin and the piano, and she had a talent for water-colour. She survived all her early struggles to enjoy a serene old age and died in 1979, aged 100 years and 4 months.

SV

6

The Untearable Suit

WHILE WANDERING along the riverside one day I found part
of a landing net. It was one of the old-fashioned wooden-hoop
types with a strong and deep net made of oiled silk. The handle
was missing. This was indeed a treasure and no thought entered
my mind that I ought to try and find out who had lost it.
Obviously it had been dropped by one of the fly-fishermen. To
me it was something I might use to try and catch fish and my one
desire was to find out how I could do this to the best advantage.

53

But first it needed a long handle and I remembered that at home there was a small pitchfork. This I thought would do well if I spread out the two tines to fit the wooden framing of the net. I knew just where to find the fork and soon the tines were spread and straightened to fit. I lashed them on securely with some twine and there I had a long-handled net which would reach out quite six feet into the river. With this I thought there might be a good chance of catching some fish while wading on the shallows.

It was high summer and the water temperature was high – warm enough to paddle and indeed to go in up to my waist if I wished. So away I went, taking the big net with me. To be on the safe side I thought it would be best to take off my shorts and in a moment these were cast down on the bank with my shoes and stockings. With a piece of string I fastened my shirt around my waist to keep the front and tail clear of the water, and with everything prepared I waded out to one of the deeper pools where a fair shoal of grayling could be seen. After chasing these upstream out of their pool I set the big net in a run between two large growths of ranunculus and then waited patiently for a grayling to swim down into it. It was absorbing and fascinating and so interested did I become that I was oblivious of all else around me. My attention was centred on one very big grayling which several times had drifted tail first down the little run so that his tail had actually crossed over the rim of the net on two occasions. Tensed, I would wait in the hope that he would drift back just a few more inches, but each time the fish seemed to sense a trap and wagged away upstream again.

Then once more the big fish drifted back. Trembling so much that I had difficulty in holding the net still, I watched as he came nearer and nearer. Still he dropped back and over the rim went his tail, then, very slowly, the whole body and his head. With a quick lift of the net I had him. There he was struggling in the meshes, a fish of quite two pounds, and, as I turned to go out to the bank with my catch, there stood a fisherman with a rod in his right hand. In the other hand were my shorts, and, holding them up, the fisherman said in a quiet voice: 'If you want these, young man, then you had better come to the Nag's Head Cottage, and bring that net and fish with you.'

There was no choice but to obey, and so, taking the string

from around my waist, I let down my shirt and put on my stockings and shoes. With the net and the grayling I followed him up to the cottage. There, feeling very conscious that a breeze was blowing my shirt about, I had to stand in front of the house where I was given a lecture on poaching. My net and the fish were taken from me and then my shorts were returned. As I scrambled to put them on, loud girlish laughter came from within the cottage. My face felt hot and, without stopping to do up the buttons, I ran out of the gate and away home. What happened to my father's pitchfork I do not know. It was never returned.

I hated new clothes. Something always seemed to go wrong whenever I was wearing anything clean or good. There was the dark-green jersey my mother had spent hours in knitting. I was proud of this because it was the right colour to merge with the greenery about the river, and it had a roll-top neck. All new clothes, shoes, and boots would be worn first of all on a Sunday. I had worn this jersey twice to Sunday school but now was the first time on a weekday. It was a Monday and on my way home from school I thought of a crow's nest which was at the top of an elm tree close beside the river upstream from our house. The nest building had hardly been completed when I had climbed to have a look at it a week before. But now I felt sure it would have eggs in it. I wanted the egg of a crow for my collection and I had promised my friends at school that I would get one each for them too. I knew it would not take long to climb the tree. It was quite an easy one.

There were four eggs in the nest. I transferred them to my cap, just behind the peak, and put it gently back on my head. The descent was made without trouble and I was quickly on my way home down the river bank. Many times I had carried eggs in my cap and they had always been quite safe. Carrying them in this way, rather than in a pocket, left one's hands free and there was far less chance of them being broken in a thoughtless moment. All would have been well on this occasion had it not been for the stile, and the weasel.

Just as I got to the stile a weasel popped out from a hole in the river bank with a baby water-vole in his mouth and went running along the bank in front of me. In a moment I was after him. Jumping up on the stile I completely forgot all about the branch one had to dodge under and the front of my head came in hard contact with it. There was a crunch. My hand flew to my cap but too late. The sticky mess of smashed eggs flowed down my face and neck, to spread all over the collar and shoulders of my new jersey. I did my best to clean it off but it was just hopeless. The yellow of the yolks spread all over the wool and was accentuated by the dark-green background.

I have not yet mentioned my mother's boiler stick. Now is the time to introduce it. This stick was one she used to lift the clothes out of the boiler in our washhouse. Originally it had been part of an ash branch from which the bark had been peeled, and it was just over two feet long and about an inch thick. The stick had been rubbed so many times on the edges of the boiler that the centre part was much thinner than the ends. It was all frayed and ragged and the wood was bleached as white as snow. When not in use this stick stood on end beside the boiler chimney. The sight of it is imprinted for ever on my memory as no doubt, at times, the shape was imprinted on my behind. Unfortunately for me, this stick always seemed to be within easy reach of my mother whenever she discovered I had been into mischief. She was washing some clothes when I appeared with my jersey all messed up with the crow's eggs and once again the stick was put to a use for which it was not intended. Boiler sticks are not used as much today by housewives. Usually they have a pair of wooden tongs to extract the clothes from boiling water. Good as they are for this purpose, I can't imagine them being of much use to mete out punishment.

Providing clothes to keep me tidy and respectable was always a problem for my mother and she was forever mending one thing or another that I had torn scrambling through a hedge or a barbed wire fence. It was a problem she thought might be solved when she read in one of the daily papers an advertisement setting out the merits of a boys' suit made of some untearable material. She might have known that there is no such thing, but at the time she thought it would be just right for me. It was not expensive. My measurements and the money were sent and in due course the suit arrived from the makers. The cloth was hard and shiny and of a brown and yellow mixture.

As usual with new clothes, I wore it first on a Sunday. The stiff material chafed my legs and wrists. My friends were all a little

envious when I told them it was untearable and a special kind of
suit my mother had got purposely for me. 'Bet it will tear,' they
said, and after Sunday school was over I was challenged to go
through a thick thorn hedge. Nothing daunted, through the
hedge I went, first forwards, then backwards, and not a tiny
snag showed on the suit. The makers were right, I thought.
What a grand suit to have!

That evening I went to show a friend a hole in a chalk-pit
where I knew a kingfisher had a nest. It was in a very awkward
place but on several occasions I had climbed to it along a ledge
where there were a few tree roots to act as handholds. The last
time, I had torn my trousers badly while wriggling through a
narrow place between two branches and I had the stick when I
got home afterwards. My friend was very thrilled to see the hole
in which the kingfisher had her nest but was not satisfied with
this. He must see into it and get a view of the eggs, or the young
ones, as the case might be.

Knowing I had been along the ledge made him all the more
determined, and so he clambered up. All went well until it came
to negotiating the narrow place between the two branches.
There he got stuck and, try as he would, he could not get free.
He could move neither forwards nor backwards and implored
me to go to his assistance. I hesitated. That last time I had torn
my trousers and got into a chalky mess and now I had on this
new suit. Still, I thought, it would not tear and I could easily
brush off the chalk before going home. With these thoughts I
scrambled up the side of the chalk-pit to where my friend was
trapped about twenty feet from the ground, and with my help
he was able to wriggle free and get down. As I turned to make
my own descent the tail of my jacket caught on a sharp project-
ing spike. It was a Norfolk-type jacket, with a vent at either side
and a kind of belt around the middle. The spike on the branch
held firmly. I turned round to try and free myself and my full
weight came on to one hand which was holding a root. With a
shower of chalk which covered me from head to foot, the root
came free. Down I went until my weight came on to the tail of my
jacket caught on the spike. There was a sound of tearing, a
sudden jerk, and down I went feet first to the bottom of the
chalk-pit.

Fortunately I landed on a pile of rotten hay and straw which broke my fall but, oh, when I looked at my jacket my heart sank within me. It is true the material had not torn but the stitches from the two vents to the shoulders had ripped apart so that the whole back of my jacket was just a loose flap. Not only this, my trousers were minus the back buttons where my braces had torn them free. While I was looking at the damage my friend came to me. 'Coo, you won't half catch it when you get home. I thought you were a good climber!' Not a word of thanks for helping him get free. 'Thought you said your suit was untearable.' And he laughed. It was too much. He was a friend no longer. With a well timed right I hit him hard and true between the eyes to stretch him out flat on his back with all the smirk and fight knocked out of him.

It was some time before I managed to pluck up enough courage to go home. I know I must have looked a ragged, dirty and pathetic little figure as I crept through the door to meet my mother and get my punishment. Perhaps it was the tragic look on my face, perhaps it was the comical side which had the appeal – I do not know. Instead of giving me the thrashing I expected and indeed deserved, to my surprise my mother burst out laughing. She laughed and she continued to laugh until I thought the sight of me had affected her brain.

'Oh!' she gasped out. 'Oh! The untearable suit. I knew it, I knew it,' she kept repeating. She laughed until she cried. 'For goodness sake go upstairs and take it off, boy. I can't bear the sight any longer.'

You can be sure I did not wait to be told a second time.

7

Disaster with a
Wasp's Nest

THE MEMORY of unpleasant things seldom lasted very long.
The magic of the riverside was always calling me and I was now
free to wander more or less at will, without much fear of being
chased by keeper or fishermen. The pool near my home was
always noted for the big fish in it but hitherto I had been afraid to
try and catch any of them. The pool was a difficult one to see into
owing to the continual swirling water coming through the open
hatches. So it was not possible to see either trout or grayling well

enough to be able to catch them with a snare. Today, for a few pence, one can get hooks and spools of fine nylon but at the time of which I write tackle such as this was not for the small boy. Indeed, nylon had not then been invented. I had to make do with an outfit of my own construction. It was crude, it is true, but it served my purpose and with it I had lots of fun. For a rod I had a nine-foot withy stick which I had peeled and allowed to dry. A length of black cotton served for a line and this was about the same length as the rod, and tied directly to the tip. The hook was a bent pin.

The fish in the pool were partly tame, for I had often fed them. A handful of small pieces of bread would soon bring the fish on to feed and with a small crusty piece on the hook I would dangle it down to the water from the bridge. Some of our fishermen of the present day would know much better how to hook and play a fish had they started their fishing career with a withy stick, cotton, and a bent pin for a hook. It was easy to see a fish take the bait, and then I would drop the top of the stick down to slack off the cotton, then flick up sharply as I saw it being drawn under. It is true I lost a number of big fish before discovering just how to handle the rod when one was on the hook. Invariably the hook would take a good hold and, keeping the rod held up almost vertically, I would let the fish pull as hard as he wanted to. My withy stick was far more supple than any split-cane, glass-fibre or steel rod made for trout and grayling fishing. When the fish was pulling hard it would bend right down until the tip almost touched the water, and then straighten again as the strain was lessened. Eventually the spring of the rod would prove the master and exhaust the fish until it came splashing to the surface. It was then just a matter of towing it to a shallow part where I could take a hold on it with my hands.

I got many fish up to a pound and a half but though I hooked others much larger they proved to be too strong. Sometimes the pin straightened, or tore free, and on some occasions the cotton would snap. In the pool was one outsized fish, a trout which might then have weighed six or seven pounds. I hooked him several times as he came surging up from deep down in the pool to snatch the bait. He was a dark bronze colour, a typical Avon trout with large dark-red spots along his sides which looked to be as large as sixpences. Each time I hooked him he would make one savage rush away from me which pulled the rod down to the water and broke the cotton.

As events proved, it would have been far better for the fishery had I caught and killed this fish at that time. We grew older together, he and I, and I saw him many times, for this fish stayed in that pool until 1932 and became a menace to all other occupants. Death sentence was then passed upon him by the secretary of the Officers' Fishing Association after we had both seen him with another trout of about one and a half pounds crosswise in his jaws. He had become a confirmed cannibal and was as bad as a big pike in any trout water. I caught him then. He weighed exactly ten pounds and, incidentally, is the largest trout I have ever seen taken from the upper Avon.

Times were very hard for anyone with a family to keep on the miserable army allowance during the latter part of the First World War, and I suspect it was as much as my mother could do to feed and clothe us all. I was too young to give much thought to this. Indeed, I fear I had little thought for anything other than fishing and being about the river valley. I had great fun trying to catch the fish in the mill-pool but it was not always trouble-free. To get the fish on the feed it was always necessary to have some bread and, though at times my mother had a few scraps to spare, often I was told that if I wanted bread to go fishing then I must go without myself. On occasions I would smuggle away a few pieces by putting them in my pockets or beneath the front of my jersey, but it was seldom I had enough to fish for any length of time at a stretch.

On my return home one day a glance at the mill-pool showed that the hatches had been closed and this was always exciting. With the hatches closed and the water shut off from the main river the pool was always quiet with no swirls or foam, and it was then quite easy to see right down to the bottom, even in the deepest part. It was only very occasionally that these hatches were closed and immediately I thought old William Pratt must be about somewhere as sometimes he used the hatches to build up a head of water with which he could flush away cut weed or other debris from the reach below. However, a good look round did not disclose his presence and an inquiry of the gardener at the Mill House brought the information that the hatches had been shut to fill a big pond, which at one time was used as a training place for army engineers. They would not be kept shut for long, he added, as the pool was almost full.

Popping indoors, I found that my mother was out. This was disappointing as I was going to ask her for some bread. I was too impatient to await her return and so, going to the bread-pan, I looked in. All there was in the pan was the bottom of a cottage loaf from which a crust had been taken. I hesitated. I knew I would get into trouble if I took bread without permission, but temptation was strong. I thought of those big fish swimming around in the pool. They might open the hatches again at any moment. It went through my mind that she would not notice if I took a thin slice, and with this thought came action. Quickly I cut a thin slice and then out for my rod.

A few crumbs from the middle of the slice brought a few fish to the surface and then I dangled in my bait. But not a fish would take. I threw in other crumbs then bits of the crust but not until the last piece of the slice had gone did a trout take the bait on my hook. I struck rather too quickly and just touched the fish before he was away taking my bait with him. That would happen, I thought, just when the fish were well on the feed; if only I had another slice of bread I felt sure I would get a good trout. Should I get some more? Once again the temptation was too strong. A second slice came from the bottom of that loaf and soon this also had gone to join the first one in the bellies of those fish. They tantalised me. They would come swirling up within inches of my bait to take pieces I threw but none made the mistake of taking the piece on the hook.

There I could see a dozen or more great big trout and grayling swimming about high in the water and once again I went to the bread-pan and came running back with a third slice of bread in my hand. Soon I was busy again. Three or four of the very biggest fish were well on the feed and taking every piece I threw in. Leaning well out, I dropped my baited hook so that it sank, and a great spotted trout headed towards it.

Then, through the golden silence and tense moments of anticipation came the voice of my mother, and in a tone I dreaded. 'Oh, so that's where the bread has gone, is it? I thought as much, you naughty boy. Didn't I tell you never to have bread without my permission?' She had known where to find me and had come prepared. A quick glance showed me the ragged fibres of the wood in the middle of the boiler stick just before it came across my shoulders. 'Indoors you rascal, and not a bite of tea shall you have. Give me that rod. I'll teach you to steal the loaf to feed those dratted fish.' In a twinkling my rod was snapped into three pieces and just as she was throwing it into the bushes she noticed my line. 'And so there's the cotton I couldn't find last week.'

Again the stick came across my shorts, as she grasped my collar. No rheumatics in her arm today, I thought, as I yelled strongly for mercy. But mercy was not forthcoming. She ran fast enough to keep within striking distance as I made a bolt for home. That was a day when I richly deserved punishment for it happened that the bottom of that loaf was all my mother had to give the whole family for tea. As she said time and again, far more than my share had gone to feed the fish in the mill-pool, and I had to watch while the others had theirs.

After this trouble my fishing with a rod and line had to be abandoned for a while. Though it was quite a simple matter to get another rod my mother flatly refused to let me have any cotton. The length she had discovered on the rod when she broke it up was the last on a reel I had found in her sewing basket, which I had taken thinking it would not be missed. Apparently it was the last bit of black she had left and she had wanted it in a hurry one day to mend a garment for a friend, who had called to see her in some distress. Though I plucked up sufficient courage to ask for bread, just to feed the fish and keep them tame, permission was refused. 'No, not another bit of bread will you have' – and she made quite sure I did not smuggle any away at mealtimes. I had never had much success when using worms and at that time had not discovered that both trout and grayling would take maggots. I found this out by accident a while later.

Looking into the pool one afternoon I could see two big trout feeding busily underwater just beneath where I was standing on the bridge. Just there, the butt of a tree stood out over the water for a yard or so. It was rotten and hollow at the end, and in a hole I could see something furry. Wondering what it could be, I got a stick and poked it into the hole, and then I saw that it was a dead barn rat. As I withdrew the stick a dozen or so maggots came tumbling out, to fall into the water just where the trout had been feeding. Immediately there was enlightenment. So that's what they were after – maggots. This knowledge was stowed away in my mind for a future date.

A while afterwards, when wandering in the other direction, I came across a part of the bank where the cattle and horses had a drinking-place. All around this was a barbed-wire fence and where the animals had been swishing their tails to keep the flies away a lot of long hairs had caught on the spikes of the wire, and had been pulled free from their tails. Some of the hairs were quite two feet in length and, on testing them, I found they were almost as strong as the best cotton I had used. Immediately my thoughts went back to fishing. Here to hand was a line, if I could join the hairs securely. Sitting down, I knotted some of the longest hairs together until I had a length of ten feet and a few pieces to spare. Tying one end to the fence I gave a sharp pull. The knots held and I had a good line. Now I could have a go for those trout I had seen feeding on the maggots.

Soon a set of tackle was made up and round to the pool I went, to see if the trout were there and to get some maggots. No trout were to be seen and when I probed into the hole I found that the maggots had gone too. All that was left was a few bones and some scraps of fur. All those preparations for nothing! It was disappointing and I felt like crying. Where could I get some maggots? A wasp buzzed around my head and dejectedly I made a swipe at it with my hat. then suddenly a thought came.

At my mother's home at the Basin, I had watched my grand-father dig out a wasp's nest and then break it open with his spade. It was the size of a small football and in it were hundreds of grubs. True, they were larger than blowfly maggots but I felt sure they would make good bait. Wasp's nests are always numerous along river banks for the queen often starts off a colony in the hole of a water-vole. I knew where there were two not far from my home. I had it in mind to kill the swarm and then dig out the nest and so, getting a spade, I ran off up river. The only way I could kill off the wasps was by drowning them, and I searched about until I found a big tin which would hold about two gallons of water.

Three times I filled this big tin and poured it down the hole of the first nest I came to, while with my hat I beat off any insects that came too near. Then, jamming the tin down tightly to prevent the escape of wasps from the nest, I stood back and waited for them all to drown. Most of the swarm must have been underground for few came from outside, and these were quickly dealt with. Ten minutes passed and then, moving forward with my spade, I turned back the tin ready to dig. So sure was I that all the wasps had been drowned that I bent forward as the tin tipped back, and quickly learned that this was a mistake.

Out of the tin and the hole the swarm came in an angry horde and in a moment they were around and on me. With a yell I ran for dear life, all the while trying to beat them off, until I had gone fully a quarter of a mile. It was without success. My legs, hands and face were stung in a dozen different places. One wasp had crawled up my shorts to sting me twice on my bottom, another went down from my neck to sting me between the shoulders. Gasping with pain and exertion, I rushed home to tell the tale to my mother.

Quickly she stripped me of all my clothes and killed the wasps which were still crawling about me. Then she rushed to the washhouse for the blue-bag and daubed each sting with it. The wet blue-bag brought immediate relief from the terrific pain but only for a short time. For hours afterwards the pain was intense and I thought I was going to die. One eye was blocked completely by the swelling of a sting beneath it and one ear was at least three times its normal size. I could not sit down and could only lie on my tummy. To bed I had to go. It was a long time before I had any desire to go fishing again. Many times since then different anglers have told me that wasp grubs are wonderful bait for fish of many kinds, as well as trout and grayling. Whether this is true I cannot say, for I have never used them myself. Such a painful lesson as the one I had in trying to get grubs was never to be forgotten. Not for all the fish in the mill-pool would I try to get others again.

8

Sunstroke, Moorhens, and Jackboots

RED HAIR and a fair skin invariably go together. My mother
had told me many times not to strip off and lie in the hot sun.
'You'll get burnt badly if you do,' she had said. And I had been
careful until one morning in late June I paid a visit to a school
friend named Harold, who lived in a cottage at Limekiln, near
Milston. This cottage was one of a row of four which stood about
a hundred yards from the river, a mile or so upstream from my
home. Harold was a boy whose inclinations were somewhat
similar to my own and he and his pal Cooky haunted the river
about Milston. At school he had told me about the hordes of
grayling there were in some pockets and pools about the shal-

66

lows near to his home. There were hundreds, he had said, and lots over two pounds. He and Cooky had been trying to snare some of them but had found them to be too difficult.

This part of the river was also in the charge of old William Pratt. Many times Harold and Cooky had been chased by the old keeper and both were well known to him. This was in the summer of 1917. The war had been on three years and the fishing people were not much concerned just then with what happened about the riverside. Most of the officers who fished this water in peacetime had far more important things to think about. We saw less and less of the keeper and no one else worried us.

All went as arranged. I made the visit to Limekiln and there met Harold and Cooky. It was a blazing hot morning – no wind and the sun shining from a clear blue sky. All I had on was a pair of shorts, a shirt and my old crow hat. I had taken with me my best wire noose on the longest stick. Together the three of us went to the shallow, to where an old withy pollard stood close beside the river. This tree was to be the viewing-point. It was an easy one to climb and at the top of the trunk there was plenty of space to stand or sit in comfort. From the top it was very easy to see into the water and a quick glance was all I needed to see that Harold had not exaggerated about the grayling. There, just opposite the pollard, was a deep pool and in this, continually on the move, were scores of fish and some I knew were well over two pounds.

We decided we would take turns with the wire and stick. Harold had first go while I watched from the tree with Cooky. The stick was hardly long enough to reach beyond the middle of the pool, but this was enough if one was patient. The fish were well aware of our presence and were agitated and would go round and round the pool. In doing this some came within easy reach. Grayling are not easy fish to snare. Time and again a fish would glide right through the wire noose. Harold would pull on the stick, but always too late. It was then decided that we should each have four pulls and then give up the stick to the next. Cooky had his turn and I had mine but still the fish eluded us. It was fascinating. Those big grayling would come swimming along almost to where the wire noose lay set upon the bottom, then glide away to just miss it on one side or the other. We would push the noose out into the direction they were swimming and try to drift the noose over one or another, but all to no purpose. It was hot. Harold took off his shirt and then Cooky did likewise. I forgot the warning my mother had given me and off came mine too, to be cast down on the bank. There the three of us were, stripped to the waist and oblivious of everything but the desire to get a grayling.

Hours passed, with all of us exposed to the broiling sun, and we caught nothing. My back felt lovely and warm as I bent forward, watching from the top of the tree. It was warm too as I stood holding the stick for the last time before going home to dinner. A big grayling, the largest in the pool, was swimming gently along and heading straight for the noose. I could see him clearly one moment, then everything went misty. I felt dizzy and only by holding fast to the tree did I stop myself from falling into the water. My tummy felt funny as though I was going to be sick.

'Coo, I feel bad,' I said to my friends. 'I nearly fell in just then, I nearly fainted I'm going home.' Funny how your thoughts go to home the moment you feel unwell. Putting on my shirt and with a promise to see the other two another day, I left them. My recollections of my return home are very, very hazy. My head ached, my back burned, and every now and then I had to sit down and rest.

The week which followed was one of agony. My mother said I had narrowly escaped sunstroke. My back was burned from shoulders to waist and all the skin peeled off. I had to stay home from school and I had no inclination to go out beside the river, but once the skin had peeled off my back I was quite comfortable again.

◇　　　◇　　　◇

Autumn came and it was after hearing my mother talk about having moorhens roasted for dinner when she was a girl that I decided I would try and catch some. Moorhens were always plentiful, and a score or more could often be seen in the long meadow between the sidestream and the main river, where they fed on the short sweet grass and other herbage. Many a time I had seen their runs, where they popped beneath the bottom strand of barbed wire on the fence by the stream, and then on into the reeds and rushes. I thought that if I made up some snares with fine wire I could tie them on the fence and perhaps catch some of the birds. The more I thought about it the more the idea appealed to me and so I asked my mother if I could try. She was quite pleased. Yes, I could set my snares and she would prepare and cook any moorhens I caught. But I was to be sure to keep away from the main river.

In the woodshed was a length of army telephone wire used in field work that I had brought home thinking it might be useful for pike snares. This was cable, and was made up of seven strands of very fine steel wire, with a copper core. Soon I had unravelled this and made up a dozen snares, then away up and along the stream. Though fine, the steel wire was brittle and not very easy to arrange in the runs, but by persevering, and with the help of a few short sticks of withy, I managed to set the snares in the runs which were used most frequently. When this was done I went back home and waited an hour before returning to see if any birds were caught. It was disappointing. Some moorhens had been along the runs for three of the snares had been drawn and two others knocked to one side, but not a single one had been caught.

I set them all again and went back home for another spell of waiting only to hear that my mother wanted something from the draper's store at Durrington. When I was tearful, and demurred about going, she said, 'You are a silly boy. Those moorhens won't come out any quicker if you wait here. The time will go much faster if you have something to do.' So away to Durrington I went but all the while I had visions of the moorhens heading into my snares.

As so often happens when one is in a hurry, the shop was full of customers, mostly women. The small boy was disregarded while the shopkeeper chattered on about print, crash, bodices and petticoats, until I felt like screaming out my requirements. But at long last I was served and home I went at a run, to be greeted with. 'You have been a long time,' just as though I had been playing about instead of doing my utmost to be quick. As I glanced up the meadows from our back door I could see two black dots moving about. 'Some moorhens are out, Mum,' I said. 'I bet there's one in my wires. Can I go and see?' 'Oh drat the boy,' she grumbled. 'If it isn't fish, it has to be something else to take you up the riverside. Yes, get along do, and give me a bit of peace.'

As I approached, the moorhens ran towards the stream and straight towards my snares. Running fast and watching, I saw a flutter of black wings beneath the fence. One was caught, I knew, and I hared across the meadow in a short cut. More haste meant less speed. My foot caught in a tuffet of bull-grass and headlong I went sprawling into a muddy ditch. I got covered in mud, all over my hands and knees and down the front of my jersey. I scrambled up unhurt and there to my joy was a moorhen caught by the neck. Quickly I killed it and reset the snare, then on to look at the others. Two more moorhens were caught and, full of it all, I carried them home.

I thought I would be in trouble for getting dirty but for once this was overlooked. My mother was quite pleased to have the moorhens. As she said, they would make us all a nice Sunday dinner, especially if I could manage to get one or two more. Once again I heard all about the nice dinners she had as a girl and how my granny prepared and cooked them. 'You must pluck them tomorrow,' she said, 'and I'll get them ready to stuff and to roast. Though I made two more visits before dark, no more birds were caught in the snares. I decided to leave them for the night and have a look first thing in the morning, before going to school.

Morning came but there was no chance to go up the meadow. We were late for school as it was. The moorhen snares must wait till dinner time, even though I could see several black dots about on the grass. I was first away when we were dismissed at twelve o'clock but as I came within sight of our front door I could see someone talking to my mother. It was the gardener from the Mill House. 'Oh, there you are, Frank,' my mother said on catching sight of me. 'Mr Leveridge wants to talk to you.'

Wondering what I had done wrong, I stood waiting. 'These are yours, aren't they?' he said, with a severe look on his face, as he brought a bundle of snares from behind his back. 'You set them along the fence yesterday for moorhens over by the old drawn. I saw you do it. Well, you won't set any more there. This morning I heard a great commotion going on along the stream and when I got there I found five of my ducks all caught by the neck, and one moorhen. The ducks were all alive and have come to no harm, but don't you go putting any more snares along there or there will be trouble for you, my boy.' I said I was sorry, and my mother made her apologies too.

'Yes, I am sorry. As I told you, Mr Leveridge, it was my fault for letting him put the snares up there, but I hadn't thought about your ducks. I'll see it doesn't happen again. Thank you for the moorhen. He caught three there yesterday and this one with those will make a good dinner for them all.'

So ended my attempt to catch moorhens for our dinners and this was a pity because we all very much enjoyed our meal on the Sunday. Stuffed and roasted moorhens make a very tasty dish.

◇   ◇   ◇

This incident was soon forgotten by the old gardener. He had a lot of tame ducks to look after at that time and many of them would range far up the river after being released from the pens each morning. On occasions some would stay out all night and in consequence he was losing their eggs. He asked my mother if she could spare me of an evening to go up the river and chase the ducks home. He would be pleased to give her a few eggs as payment. Of course I was more than eager to do this. It gave me a good excuse to go as much as a mile or more and I was very pleased when my mother said I could go. A few eggs would be very welcome, she added.

The meadows were very wet and overflowing to the river when I went for the ducks one evening. The drowner had opened the hatches to irrigate the meadows in the morning, and water from the big carrier had spread gradually all about the short grass, going from runnel to ditch and from ditch to drawn, or to the main river. In jumping the ditches and going through the rough herbage along the river bank I got wet through almost to the knees. On my return to the Mill House with the ducks, this was soon noticed by the old gardener. 'Looks as though you've got pretty wet, Frank boy,' he said. 'What have they done up there, got the water in the meadows again? Old Hooper drowning his meadows, I suppose. T'others don't do much of it now. It was mighty wet up there last year about this time when I had to go once or twice. What's your mother going to say about they shoes of yours? You tell her I am sorry, but I got the very thing for you at home. There's a pair of leather knee-boots there that will just about fit you. I'll bring them along tomorrow and you can try them on. Tell your mother I'll try and fix you up with something to keep you clean and dry.'

The old gardener was as good as his word. When I got home from school at midday my mother gave me the boots. 'Here are those boots Mr Leveridge brought for you. You must thank him very much when you see him. They ought to be just the thing for you to go out in after those ducks.' Just the thing they were, too. Though a trifle big, they came to my knees, and in a few moments I was in the river to see if they were watertight. They were. No more would I have to be careful and have to find all the dry places. No more hidings for getting my shoes and stockings dirty. I could go right to the river edge and in the water where it was shallow. I would have kept them on during dinner if my mother had not insisted on my putting them in the woodshed. Indeed, I would have worn them to school, so proud was I. Jackboots! I had a pair of leather jackboots. I would be the envy of all the other boys.

My mother just couldn't understand a boy's heart. She didn't realise that those old jackboots meant far more to me than a new suit, that the thrill I would have in wearing them was akin to the thrill she herself had when going out to friends wearing a new hat or coat for the first time. Shabby and crinkled though they were, high-legged boots and waders were part of a fisherman's outfit. In the back of my mind was the thought that these would be useful for more purposes than chasing ducks home.

After school was over I clumped off round to see the old gardener. As he saw me approaching he came to attention and brought his hand smartly to a salute. 'Avast, ye lubbers,' he bawled out. 'Make way for the captain in his sea-boots. Captain, Sir, I greet thee.' I laughed for I could not make head or tail of his tomfoolery, and then thanked him for the boots. But for ever afterwards to him I was Captain, no matter if I was wearing the boots or not.

No doubt I looked a queer little fellow plodding along. The soles of the boots were heavily nailed and they were rather heavy. My mother had not thought to tell me to change my stockings for some old ones. Those I had on were nearly new. The ducks were much farther up the river than usual and I had walked quite three-quarters of a mile before finding them. By then my legs were tired and my heels felt a bit sore as they slipped up and down in the boots at every stride. The journey back was even more tiring and my heels seemed to get worse – indeed, they were hurting. Several times I stopped to rest, but finally I got the ducks home and into their pen.

'Well, Captain, how are the boots?' the old gardener asked. 'Didn't get your feet wet today, did you?' 'Oh no, thank you, Mr Leveridge. They're jolly good. My mother was pleased when they fitted me, and said they were just the thing.'

With half a dozen eggs in my hat I left the old man and went home, but tears had come to my eyes before I got to the door and these my mother quickly noticed, as I went inside to give her the eggs and sit on a chair. 'What's the matter, my son? What are you crying for? Have you been up to some mischief?' Strange, wasn't it? Mischief, the first thought that entered her mind. Just as though a boy couldn't cry without having been in mischief. 'No, Mum,' I answered. 'I haven't done anything wrong. My heels hurt.'

In a moment her face softened and the tone of her voice grew more gentle. 'Those big boots, here, let me pull them off.' In a moment the trouble was exposed. There in the heels of both my stockings were holes big enough for me to put my fist through, and there on my heels were two big blisters.

'Oh, just look at those new stockings, those I bought only last Saturday. Oh, you naughty boy, you won't have any to go to school in tomorrow. I might have known. I'll burn those old jackboots. Old Leveridge ought to have more sense than give them to you. You won't wear them again. I won't let you go after his silly old ducks.' These, and a few more exclamations, came from my mother in a long string, and then she seemed to remember the blisters, and bent to have a second look. 'Oh dear, you poor little chap. How ever did you manage to walk with heels like that?' Why ever didn't you take them off when you found your heels were getting sore?' Gently she pulled off my stockings and bathed my heels in warm water. Then she pricked both blisters with a needle to let out the water gathered beneath the skin. Soon some soothing ointment was applied and then a bandage on each foot.

As it happened I did not want my stockings for school the next day, or for several other days. My heels were much too sore for me to wear my school boots, or Sunday shoes, for neither were large enough to be comfortable. It was to be many weeks before I wore the jackboots again but never did I get the same thrill as on that first appearance.

9

'Alfy's in the Water, Alfy's Gone'

YOU MAY THINK that all the incidents in my young life were coupled with either pain or punishment. Perhaps this is why I recollect them so clearly. Most of them were, for trouble dogged me wherever I went or whatever I did. I was always restless, as restless as the river I loved, always ready to do something different, to try out some new idea and find out why things happened. It is true I had punishment, but far less than I really deserved, and usually the pain I suffered was brought about by my own thoughtlessness or foolishness. Had my mother known one half the things I did I fear she might have given up in despair.

75

My mother was to have another baby and arrangements had
been made for a woman in the village to come and look after her
and the family during the time she was 'lying in', as it was called.
The woman was Mrs Spratt and she was, I think, some relation
to the old keeper who looked after the river. He had changed his
name from Spratt to Pratt. The relationship was not a close one,
or if it was the families had little to do with each other, but this is
in passing. Spratt was her name, and she had a son, two or three
years younger than myself. His name was Freddie. When she
came to look after my mother she brought Freddie with her, and
it was my job to see that he did not get into mischief. You may
well laugh at that remark, but I had promised my mother that I
would be good, and it was a promise I had every intention of
keeping.

The Spratts lived at the far end of Bulford village, which was
well away from the river, and indeed from any stream. So it was
something very new for Freddie to be at the riverside. From the
start it fascinated him. Our garden runs beside the river and not
more than ten yards downstream are the big hatches which
control and regulate the flow. For a day or two Freddie was quite
content to stay with me in the garden, where we fished for
minnows and paddled in the shallow, to find bullheads, loaches
and crayfish. I showed him the caddis crawling about on the
stones and the little nymphs of the fish flies. We caught shrimps
and creepers and lots of other things, and kept them in jam-jars
for him to take home. But he was not satisfied. He wanted a
boat.

Boats were not of much interest to me – playing boats, I mean
– but I had an old one in the woodshed that I had chopped into
shape from a log of wood. This I had fitted with a sail made from
a handkerchief. I had hidden it after my mother had asked about
the handkerchief, as of course I ought not to have used it for
such a purpose. It was still where I had hidden it, though the sail
had got rather black with coal dust. The boat had not been used
much because, at the time when I had a craze for sailing the
thing, I had no string long enough to let it float far on the water.
This was still the problem, and though I searched everywhere
for string, and asked Mrs Spratt if she could find some, none was
forthcoming. Then I remembered the cricket bat.

In his younger days my father had been a very enthusiastic

cricketer, and at times had played in matches with some of the Hill family. But I understood that my mother had not approved of some of the things he did after matches and at last he gave it up. One of his bats was in an old cricket bag with a pair of pads and batting gloves, and this hung from the roof at one end of the woodshed. I had been told never to play with this bat but on many occasions I had looked at it. I didn't want it now to play with, but around the handle was a binding of fine black twine. Once or twice in the past I had been very tempted to have this for a fishing line, but had hesitated, knowing my father would be very angry when he found out. But now – well, Dad was in the army and away. He wouldn't want the bat when home on leave. I'd just take the twine for today, and then wind it back on again when we had finished with the boat.

I got the bat and cut the top of the binding, then spun off the yards of twine and rolled it on to a stick. There was plenty of length to let the boat sail almost to the hatches. Tying the free end to the boat, back to the river I went to Freddie. He was delighted, I gave him the roll of twine, put the boat in the water, pushed it out, and then stood by to watch as it sailed away with the current. Freddie would pay out the twine to the end, then pull the boat back upstream and let it drift again. He was quite happy while I amused myself with some big beetles I had in a little mud pond and in watching some caddis grubs I had pulled from their cases trying to make themselves another home.

A cry from Freddie made me look up with a start. The boat had pulled free from the twine and was drifting down towards the hatches. I rushed off at once to get one of my wiring sticks from the hedge, and got back just in time to see a great splash just where the water speeded up to go through the controls. It was Freddie. I saw him come to the surface and then go down, to disappear beneath an open hatch, and I knew he would be washed through to the deep mill-pool below.

Yelling at the top of my lungs for help, I raced to the pool and there shouted even louder. The gardener and the chauffeur from the Mill House came running to me, and quickly I told them what had happened. We watched the swirling water in the pool but saw nothing. One of them ran to look above the hatches but there was no sign of him there. Panic-stricken, we again watched the pool. Then suddenly there was a shout from the gardener: 'There he is, Chalmers, clinging to the hatch!' In a moment the chauffeur had jumped the wall to the concrete apron behind the hatches, just in time to catch Freddie as his hands slipped from the hatch and he swirled with the racing water towards the pool.

Fortunately all this happened without the knowledge of Mrs Spratt or my mother and perhaps, knowing how things were in my home, the gardener and chauffeur made light of the incident when they took Freddie in. He was wet through, of course, but a little while later was none the worse for his ducking. We learned from him that he had grasped the hatch as he was being swept beneath it and had managed to hold on. It was very fortunate for him, and indeed for all concerned, that the hatch was up high enough for him to pass beneath it. Had it been open only a few inches he would have been sucked down to the bottom and there trapped and drowned, for this had happened to one of my father's brothers when he was young. Had he been washed on through to the deep pool he might well have drowned there, despite the prompt appearance of the two men in response to my calls for help.

This incident remains very clear in my memory, though for once there was no unpleasant ending in it for me. But when later on my mother was told, she recalled a very similar episode, when my oldest brother fell in and did go through the hatches into the mill-pool when the river was in flood. I was credited with having saved his life.

To me the incident is a vague memory, though some details still remain vivid. My brother and I were playing with Yerda, the daughter of the same chauffeur who pulled out Freddie Spratt, for at that time they lived in the Mill House as caretakers. I remember we were on the bank, just upstream from the hatches, and all three of us were pulling off dock leaves and dropping them into the water to watch as they were swept to the open hatches. The water was high and dirty. It is possible there had been a heavy storm, for this was in the spring, not the winter when the river was usually high. I recollect Yerda having a stick and my brother taking it from her to move a leaf that had caught on the bank. He must have leaned too far forward. In he went head first, to disappear with a great splash into the racing water. I was not three years old then, but can remember crying and running to my mother shouting:

'Alfy's in the water, Alfy's gone. Alfy's gone through the hatches.'

Out of the house rushed my mother, with me just behind, still crying. What she had in mind I cannot say, but she knew my brother Alf might still be in the mill-pool, and she ran in that direction. As she tore out of the gateway, my father came riding down the causeway towards her on his bicycle, and in a moment he was told. I can still see him as he threw his bicycle to the ground and raced to the pool. As he ran, he must have seen my brother in the swirling water. Without hesitating he cleared the four-foot wire fence at the edge with a great jump and went feet first into the water. Up he came to the surface and I could see he had my brother in his arms, and with a great struggle he got to the bank and landed. From this time onward I can remember little more, except some time later having to go to bed with my brother to keep him company. Some years later I learned that Alf was unconscious when Dad got him out, and that both he and my mother thought he was dead. Apparently the girl Yerda had run home and said nothing about the accident. Had it not been for me the river would certainly have claimed my brother as a victim. Had my father not returned earlier than usual from work, who knows what might have happened? Only in later years did I realise that my father had risked his own life – he could not swim a stroke. The water in the pool at that time was between eight and nine feet deep.

◇　　◇　　◇

Swimming was something I learned to do very early in life. My mother encouraged us all to learn, and for me it was always enjoyable. She would never let us go into bathe until the first of June. Then, seemingly, no matter what the weather, we could go and swim. My mother had some of the old-fashioned ideas about the seasons, maybe passed on to her by her parents. May was supposed to be a treacherous month and, even if it was very hot, the river water was not considered to be warm enough for bathing.

Yes, I loved it. Diving and swimming underwater was a favourite pastime with me, and when I learned that I could keep my eyes open I really felt happy. Swimming along near to the bottom I saw all kinds of different creatures in their natural habitat, and I was always amused to see the crayfish in their holes along the banks. I would see a horny head and claws, with two black eyes, then touch the long antennae with a finger and watch the big crustacean go quickly backwards into the hole and out of sight. Sometimes I managed to catch one and bring it to the surface.

It was while swimming under water that I learned of some of the hiding-places of trout in deep pools, and afterwards could well understand how easy it must be for an otter to get a fish when he wants one. In one pool there was a hollow beneath the bank, right at river-bed level. In this hollow I could always find a trout. Jutting out from the bank, a foot or so above the hollow, was the root of a long-dead tree. It made a fine handhold. I would dive down, grasp the root with my left hand, and then quite easily take a trout from the hollow with my right hand. I had fun watching them dart away in panic after being released. Occasionally I would show off, would go down and catch a fish, then take it to land to show my friends, who were not quite so keen to be near to the river bed in deep water.

10

The Great Eel

EELS WERE VERY numerous in the Avon when I was a boy
and often when hunting the river for pike I would see some lying
about the river bed or feeding in the weeds. Eels are not fish
which scare easily like trout, grayling or coarse fish. In this
respect they are somewhat similar to pike. When I found one
lying on the bottom there was always the chance that it would
remain to give me a chance to try for it with the snare. The
trouble was that they would always lie with their heads touching
the bottom and for the most part were scared when a part of the
wire touched their noses. Eels can move backwards almost as
quickly as forwards and this is what usually happened each time
I tried to get a noose over their heads and along the body. I
would try putting the noose over the tail and working it up to the

mid-part of the body but with no better result. The fish would feel the wire and away it would go.

Occasionally, however, I would come across some which were feeding amongst a shoal of spawning minnows. Eels are very fond of the tiny eggs of minnows and they will spend hours amongst a shoal, sucking up the eggs from the gaps and crevices in the gravel. I have caught them when they have had as much as an egg-cupful of the minnow spawn in them, which would represent many thousands of these tiny eggs. Many times I have sat and watched them as they moved from place to place over the river bed. For some reason the minnows are not afraid and will swarm about, around, and over the eels, and spawn within inches of their noses.

When eels were occupied in this way some could be caught with a snare but one had to be patient. The best way I found was to put the snare a few inches in front of one and then wait until he wriggled along and through it. However, to catch an eel with a snare needs perfect timing and judgement, for unless one can pull on the stick to tighten just when the wire is at the point of balance the eel will slip from the noose before a landing can be made. One has to pull sharply even when the wire is amidships, so to speak, and to be very quick in swinging the fish to land. Even then the catch is not certain, for should one escape from the noose into wet or long grass or other herbage, it meant quite a scramble to get a hold on it and make a kill. Many times I got one out only to find it disappear into the hole of a water-vole or into a mole run, or to have to go chasing after one which went wriggling through the grasses.

I once disputed the popular opinion that eels can travel over dry land from one water to another. This is impossible if the land really is dry, but in wet grass an eel can travel along at a great pace. Put them down on really dry land and they are helpless. As soon as the skin of an eel becomes dry its movement in any direction is very limited and he will remain in the one place and die even though water may be only a few yards away.

I remember one which did a journey in record time and I always think of it when people start to argue with me about eel migration. This eel was feeding, as I have just described, amongst a shoal of minnows. He was a fish of quite a pound, perhaps more. As he wriggled along the gravel and into my snare I gave a strong pull and a swing, with the wire, as I thought, at the point of balance. High into the air he went and then slipped free of the noose just above my head. The momentum of the swing sent him sailing up still higher to describe a perfect arc, and then he dropped with a splash into the middle of a stream which was quite fifty yards behind me. Though I dashed immediately to the stream, there was no sign of him. No doubt he was hidden in the weedbeds wondering just how he had made such a journey in the heat of a summer day. And this, incidentally, is the first and only time I have seen an eel leave one river to go to another over dry land.

The mill hatches near my home were occasionally closed to fill the bathing pond. When this happened all the water of the river was diverted to another outlet, with the result that the shallows at the tail of the pool were drained almost dry. There were a few exceptions in the form of small pockets and pools. Usually the water drained away so quickly that numbers of different creatures became trapped in the small pools, where, if they were not disturbed, they would be quite safe until the hatches were lifted and the flow commenced again. At such times this shallow was a favourite hunting-ground for me, and extremely fascinating, because I never knew what I might find there. I would take with me a bucket and an old carving fork.

The main purpose of this fork was catching eels in the shallows, for often I would find some trapped in the pools. In one pool, a little deeper than the others, was an old sheet of corrugated iron, about five feet long and thirty inches wide. Beneath this I was always certain to find something of interest. Lots of the river creatures like to hide in dark places whenever there is a threat of danger. In the hollow beneath this sheet of iron there would always be a horde of crayfish, bullheads and loaches, and sometimes a trout or two. Invariably there would be an eel.

I would lift the corrugated sheet very carefully from one side and peer beneath it. If an eel was there, I would deal with him first of all. To do this I would push the fork down until it was just above the back of the fish behind the pectoral fins. Then a sharp thrust would pin the eel to the river bed, where I would hold it firmly until all struggles ceased. Then, putting two fingers beneath the eel, one at each side of the prongs of the fork, I could lift up the eel and drop him into my bucket.

Usually these eels were small ones of about half or three-quarters of a pound, and were quite easy to handle. One day, however, I had a surprise for when I lifted up the iron sheet there beneath it was the biggest eel I had ever seen. His head, far bigger than my fist, came pushing out from beneath one end of the iron before I had lifted it clear of the water, and for a moment I thought it was the head of a big black trout. As I slowly lifted the sheet higher I could see him clearly. What a monster he looked! At once I could see that it was no trout but a huge eel with a body quite thirty inches long and as big round as my leg below the knee. What a whopper! Gently I lowered the sheet back to its former position and stood for a few moments to consider. Excitement gripped me. Could I catch him with my fork or should I get a snare and try to get him with that? I was afraid that, after disturbing him as I had, if I left to get a wire he would be gone while I was away. So I decided to spear him with my fork. I would dig the fork through just at the back of his head and that I hoped would kill him.

Once more I lifted up the corrugated sheet. He was still there in the same place. Then his great head came nosing along towards my bare toes and stopped. I pushed the fork down towards him with my right hand and then hesitated. Would I be strong enough to hold him down with one hand after I had stabbed him? No, I must use both hands – but how? I needed one to hold up the iron. A short length of a stick caught my eye. Yes, that would do to prop up the sheet. Lowering the iron once more, I got the stick.

Sticking my carving fork down into the gravel within easy reach, I lifted the iron for the third time. The big eel did not move and carefully I put the stick upright and balanced the sheet against it. I must admit I was scared as I took the fork in both hands and pushed it towards the back of the big eel's head. My hands trembled as I paused just a moment to make sure of my aim, then down I thrust and pressed with all my weight.

In a moment it was very obvious that I had failed to pierce a vital spot. As I pressed down hard so the body and tail of the great fish coiled around the fork handle and then up my arms. Water splashed up over my head and I could hear the points of the fork grating in the gravel. Again and again the big eel coiled and uncoiled and the great tail came sweeping across my face and neck, and over the front of my jersey. I held down grimly. The stick holding up the corrugated sheet was swept to one side and the iron fell across my left leg, making a long gash from which the blood ran into the water. But I hardly felt it.

Eels have terrific strength in their long sinuous bodies and this was an outsize one for the Avon. His struggles never ceased. My arms began to tire and I knew I was not strong enough to hold him. With a great effort, which tore the fork from my hands, he got free. Over the tail of the small pool he went, with the fork still embedded in his shoulders, to where a small stream of water led away down the centre of the shallow. As fast as I could run I went after him. Again I grabbed the fork and pinned him down but a second time he got free and now left me with the fork in my hands. Away once more, wriggling and slithering towards the deeper water by the bridge. I cut him off and made another stab which drove the fork through his back, but I could not hold him. With a tremendous wriggle which sent me off balance so that I sat backwards in the water, the big eel shot over a weedbed and into the deep. There, with slow sinuous movements he went on, to disappear for ever from my sight. Only then did I comprehend that I had lost him.

I cried. Well, who could have helped crying? My hands were sore, my arms ached and my leg was now painful. I was wet through with my arms covered in blood and slime. And then I looked at my jersey. Eel slime was all over the front of it. I could feel my face and neck stiffening and a touch with my hand was enough to know why. With a sinking heart I got my bucket and went home.

It was useless trying to explain that I had been having a fight with a monstrous eel. My mother just could not understand. There was I, with my heart almost broken through the loss of this monster, but my mother was concerned only because I had got wet and slimy. Still, I soon got over the thrashing I had. The worst part was having the dried slime cleaned from my face and neck.

11

The End of Boyhood

THE END of my freedom and boyhood ramblings at the riverside came soon after the First World War was over. My father was discharged from the army at the end of 1918 and came home. For a while I was subjected to some of the discipline he himself had experienced during his first few weeks in the service and which, later as an NCO, he had drilled into his subordinates. My father had it in his mind that the river was still preserved and looked after as it had been before the start of hostilities, and was horrified when he learned of some of the escapades I had been at during his absence. He still thought of me as his one interested son who was happy to tag along behind him. How very wrong he was!

The fishing authorities, now that peace was established, made plans to restore the river to better sporting trim, and once again old William Pratt began to appear far more regularly about Bulford. A second keeper was employed and he, to make matters as bad as they could be, came to lodge with our next-door neighbours. He took his job very seriously and haunted the river from daybreak till dark. To him had been passed a some-what exaggerated record of my previous activities. He was to see that I had no chance to fish and, indeed, had orders to chase me from the riverside whenever the occasion arose.

As I think of it now, I feel sure the trout-fishing people made a bad mistake by making this decision to banish me from the river. Though it is true that I caught some trout, grayling and other fish while having a free hand, so to speak, during the latter part of the war, the few I caught with my crude tackle were not to be compared to the numbers I saved. I killed scores of pike, far more in fact than the keeper. I know plenty were still left in the fishery but there would have been many more and still fewer trout but for my constant efforts with my snare and stick. Each pike I killed saved a yearly loss of at least fifty trout and hundreds of other fish as well. Had the fishing authorities given only a little consideration they might have felt they owed me a debt of gratitude, rather than the reverse.

Still, there it was. In their eyes, and in the eyes of the keepers they employed, I was an undesirable character, a menace to their sport. My father, who at that time stood a little in awe of all officers, gave me instructions I knew better than to disobey. My fishing tackle was all destroyed and I was not to go near the river unless it was in his company.

In the spring of 1920 I left school. I had been thirteen the previous autumn and having, with the others of my own age, reached and passed the highest standard at our school, I was allowed to leave with a special permit. The time had come when I was old enough to work and earn a little money to help clothe and feed me. For this the joys of the riverside had to be put aside. Gone for me, as I thought for ever, was the thrill I always had when preparing for some new adventure. Wistfully I would look upstream from the back door of our house before leaving for work and I would gaze deeply into the mill-pool as I passed on my way to my job. Deep-rooted in my heart was a love of the running stream, a love of the valley and all there that nature had to offer. I did not know then that a life on the river would open up for me, that the joys and thrills of my boyhood days would be few in comparison with those I would have in later years.

For this was to come. Five years were to pass. Then, at the age of eighteen, came the chance for which my heart had been yearning, and I started my life as a river keeper.

Today there are other boys at the riverside, boys who are just as full of mischief and fun as I was myself. But they will grow up, even as I did, and in time perhaps their children will come to the valley too, to have their joys and sorrows. For the old Avon flows gently on. Throughout all the seasons of the year it winds its way towards the sea, gently chuckling now and then as it passes over some gravelly shallow, chuckling, I think, because it knows the great fascination there is beneath those gleaming waters, a fascination which from time to time will clutch at the heart of a boy and hold him captive for evermore.

PART TWO

Manhood

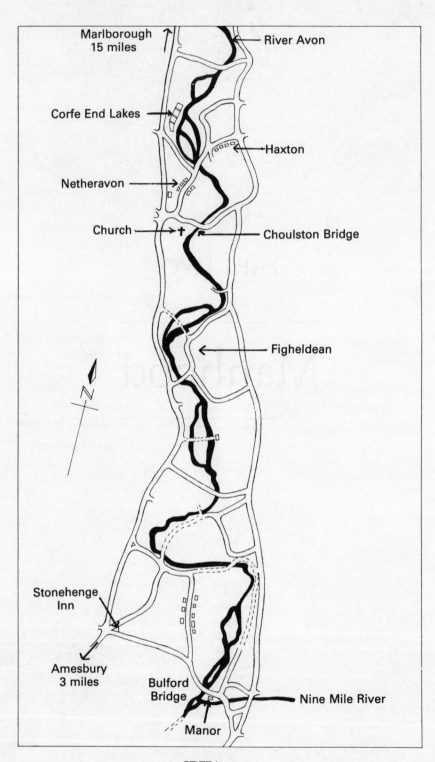

Marlborough
15 miles

River Avon

Corfe End Lakes

Haxton

Netheravon

Church

Choulston Bridge

Figheldean

Stonehenge
Inn

Amesbury
3 miles

Bulford
Bridge

Nine Mile River

Manor

SDFFA water

12

Sawyer in his Teens

*After leaving school at thirteen, Sawyer went to
work on a farm at Bulford Leas, in the valley of the
Nine Mile River, a tributary of the Avon which
joins the main river at Bulford. These two tales are
related to that time.*

A meeting of Two Redheads

C–LOCH–C–LOCH–C–LOCH. I knew at once that the sound
was made by a cock pheasant though I was quite two hundred
yards away. The call came at intervals from a patch of about half
an acre of dried rushes in the valley near the stream.

I listened carefully until I was reasonably sure where the bird
was. It was midday on a day in December – my dinner hour and
my hour of freedom from duties on the farm where I worked at
that time. I was nearly fourteen years old then, and every fine

91

day I quickly ate my dinner and hastened to the valley to hunt.

This valley didn't belong to the farm where I worked, but lay to one side of it. Parts of it were continually under my observation during working hours, and I marked down any movement of interesting creatures. A tiny stream twisted and turned through the lowest parts, and on either side of the valley was a sprawly thorn hedge. Other bushes dotted here and there amongst dense patches of rushes withered with the frost, clumps of dead brambles and the rotted trunks of fallen trees made humps which rose above the rubbish. The valley had the appearance of neglect, a haunt for wild animals and birds, and it was an ideal hunting ground.

My weapon was a catapult and my bullets rounded lumps of lead. But though I was barely fourteen years old I was quite strong enough to drive a shot both speedy and accurate, and I usually managed to kill something worthy of the pot.

Nothing gave me greater pleasure than to wander at will in this valley. Though alone, I was always happy, searching the bushes and scrub for a squatting rabbit or a hare, stalking a duck or a moorhen or perhaps a covey of partridges. Sometimes I'd wait under the thorn bushes for wood-pigeons to come and feed on the ivy berries and haws.

Occasionally there was a trout to chase about the stream or the track of an otter to follow. My dinner hour was always too short and often I had to run hard to get back in time.

The call of a cock pheasant was an unusual one to be heard in this valley – pheasants at that time rarely lived long enough to develop a call. The sound came as a surprise and something of a thrill. To me came memories of the last one I had killed – one I had found with a broken wing a year before which I had chased through the bushes and rubbish for a quarter of a mile before I got it. My mother cooked it on the following Sunday and we had it for dinner. It was good, too, and I wanted to taste another.

C–loch–c-loch. Again the call came to me and quickly I began to stalk. As I gradually approached I began to wonder what was alarming the pheasant, for undoubtedly it was an alarm call, and then I heard also the chattering of a jenny wren in a bush close by. Must be a stoat or a weasel there, I thought, and hoped that whatever it was it would keep the pheasant occupied until I could get near enough to have a shot at it. Quickly I crept through the rushes on my stomach with my catapult in hand and the roundest lump of lead I had in the pouch.

Still the call of the cock came at steady intervals to guide me, and I knew just where he was. I knew he wasn't more than five yards away – in fact, near enough for me to hit – but try as I would I couldn't see him. Between us and lying end on to me was the trunk of a large fallen tree. I knew the pheasant must be somewhere near the other end of it. I flattened to the ground and moved as silently as a snake to the tree-trunk and through the tall dead rushes along one side of it.

I peered cautiously through a light screen of vegetation and round the end of the trunk. There was the pheasant, not six feet away, his rigid head and bluey-black neck showing plainly above some fallen sedges. I could only see one eye and this seemed to be staring with a set expression straight towards me, and even as I watched his beak opened and another call sounded.

I eased my head gently forward and began to raise my catapult, and then I got one of the biggest surprises of my life. For from the other side of the tree-trunk the head of a dog fox appeared and for a moment we stared into each other's eyes at a distance of about two feet. In that brief moment I saw a vicious look appear in the eyes of the fox, a look which changed immediately to one of puzzlement. My head at that time was as red as the head of any fox (my hair, an unruly shock, was probably in a state of disorder after crawling so far through the rubbish) and I was hatless. But that brief look was enough for me. I had a horror of foxes at that time. I yelled and scrambled to my feet. Everything happened at once – with a kind of snarl the fox leapt towards the pheasant, the cock rocketed straight up into the air, and I dashed in the opposite direction as fast as my legs would carry me.

Without question the fox and I had been stalking the same prey and we were both using the same cover to do so. The pheasant must have known for a long time that the fox was stalking him, as it was his alarm call that had guided me, but I think he was a lucky bird. I shouldn't have missed his head at six feet and had I not been there to yell I feel sure the fox wouldn't have missed either.

Thinking of it afterwards, I couldn't understand why neither the pheasant nor the fox sighted or scented me, or for that matter why they didn't hear me. I came to the conclusion that both wild creatures were so intent upon each other that my approach was unnoticed. Somehow, I think that when the fox saw my red head peering round the tree-trunk he thought I was another of his kind with the same intention. Well – I suppose in a way I was, but I often wonder what would have happened had I managed to keep control of myself.

Outwitting the Hunt

Actually I went to the cover to see if I could get a couple of pigeons, but I had no right to do even this. I was poaching and at that time anything that came along was fair game. I suppose I should have known better, but I wasn't more than fifteen and nothing suited me better than to be amongst the wildlife. I hunted for the sheer joy of doing it and not for what I could get out of it. Though I had several times asked permission to shoot a few pigeons I had been refused and so I took French leave and instead of killing only pigeons I killed everything I could.

It was a late afternoon in February. I had finished work at half past four and there was still an hour or so of daylight. The cover was one of about ten acres and consisted mainly of conifers, which had grown to a height of forty feet or more. Beneath them was an undergrowth of hazel bushes and blackberries. It was a favourite roosting-place for wood-pigeons, and occasionally a pheasant chose the place in which to spend a night.

I had my ·22 rifle with me – a tiny weapon, but very accurate up to about thirty yards. It was ideal for potting pigeons from the tops of the conifers where they usually settled for a few minutes before going into the thicker cover lower down. I quickly got three with successive shots and then, faintly away over the downs, I heard the sound of hounds. Late for them to be out, I thought. I knew it must be the harriers from the kennels in the district, as there was no meet of the foxhounds that week. The cry of hounds became louder. By the tone of the cry I knew that they had found, and were on the line of a hare. What was more, they were coming in my direction.

This made me a little uneasy. I had no wish to be discovered in the cover with my rifle. I knew only too well that the Master and some of the field were members of the syndicate which rented the shooting rights, and that discovery would mean some very awkward questions, and probably put an end to my rambles. I hesitated, undecided. I was standing in the middle of a narrow ride which twisted and turned throughout the length of the cover. As I hesitated, to my ears came the sound of hurried movements – the rustle of leaves and pine needles, the crack of a twig and the movement of dried fir cones. Then above it, clear and strong, came the cry of the hounds once more. It faded into silence, and suddenly from the bushes at one side of the ride a hare bounded into view and came fast towards me.

In a moment I was a hunter – hounds and followers forgotten. My rifle was at the ready and when the hare was about five yards distant I gave a squeak. The hare had not seen me although I stood in full view, and up he went on his hind legs. My bullet struck true in the centre of his breast and he died without a kick. Only then did I realise what I had done.

What a fool I had been – discovery now seemed certain. The hounds were not more than five hundred yards away and already I could hear the galloping horses and the shouts of the riders. I did not want to leave the hare. I knew the hounds would find it, and now I had killed it I felt it was mine. I knew also that if I took it away and hid they would still be able to follow the scent. Then I glanced up. Close to the ride was a large Scotch fir with sufficient cover at the top to hide me and many hares. Like a squirrel I went up it, my bag with the hare and the pigeons in it slung over my shoulder, and my rifle in one hand. I reached the top, hung bag and rifle over one branch, and sat, still as a statue, on another.

I could hear the hounds near the outside of the cover and the cries of the huntsman as he urged them on. Soon came a crashing of branches and dead twigs, and the deep notes of the hounds as they faithfully followed the scent of the hare through the trees. Peering through the branches of the fir I saw the leading couple burst into the ride, their jaws slavering and tongues hung to one side. Jowls to ground, they came down the ride and then gave full tongue as they reached the place where I had shot the hare. A dozen other couples were soon on the scene and joined in the chorus, probably excited by the smell of blood which had come from the bullet hole. Beneath me was an indescribable scene.

Then came the sound of galloping horses as they and their riders came swiftly down the ride, heads bent to avoid the low-hanging branches. 'They've killed, I'm sure,' I heard someone shout, and then human cries mingled with those of the hounds. 'But where's Charlie?' cried a rider. 'Have they eaten him already?' 'Can't make it out,' replied the Master. 'They act as though they've killed, but they can't have eaten him yet. They must be at fault.'

Backwards and forwards along the ride he cast the hounds, while the rest of the riders stayed beneath the tree in which I was hidden. I listened to various comments, and several things very alien to hunting hares. Several of the hounds returned once more and circled round the base of my tree. I held my breath and stayed as still as death. One great hound sniffed at the trunk and then started trying to climb. I heard his claws scratch on the bark. His action did not escape the eyes of the huntsman. 'Down, Roman, you great fool – down, Sir,' he yelled, and cut viciously at the hound with his whip. 'What are you doing? Hares don't go up trees, you idiot.'

'Ha-ha-ha,' laughed the Master. 'Charlie's beaten them. We'd better call it a day, it's too dark to go on.' To my immense relief, the hunt retreated through the trees, and as soon as the last sounds were gone I slipped quickly down the tree and raced off in the opposite direction, the bag with ill-gotten gains over my shoulder. The old hound was right, I thought, as I felt the body of the hare against my back. Hares do go up trees – and they also come down them.

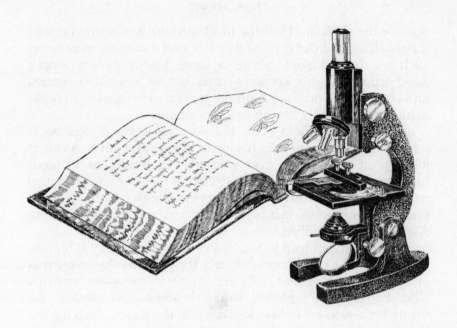

13

The Twenties and Thirties

AFTER THE FARM, Sawyer was apprenticed as a carpenter at Larkhill, about three miles from the Mill Cottage. It was the only time in his life when he did not work under the sky. He was good with his hands and learnt to use hand tools, skills which he was later to put to good use. But he would have chafed at the indoor life. Then he found work which must have been more congenial, as under-keeper on the Avon at Lake, a few miles downstream from Bulford. The head keeper was Fred Martin, a thorough and conscientious man who used to have a regular delivery of cockles and mussels at Salisbury station. He would collect them in a pony and trap, employ two village boys to remove the shells and put the meat through a mincer, and feed the result to the trout in his stews. It is said that there were never such red-fleshed trout, before or since. Martin gave Sawyer a good grounding in a keeper's work, but he was old-fashioned and would have no truck with the newfangled ideas of nymph-fishing associated with the name of Skues.

In 1928, old William Pratt, the scourge of the village boys, retired. Sawyer applied for his job as keeper and got it. As far as jobs go, it was all he ever wanted. He continued to tend, nurture, and love this 6½-mile stretch of the Avon until he died more than half a century later. It was then known as the Officer's Fishing Association, but is now the Services' Dry Fly Fishing Association or SDFFA.

For the next eighteen years, Sawyer worked quietly at his job, living always in a village a stone's throw from the river. It is important to realise that he lived not only by the river, but *in* it – weed-cutting and repairing banks, bridges, and hatches. All through these years he was looking into the water, studying the fish and the insects, observing their life-cycle, and making careful notes.

His wages in the thirties were £2 per week, and out of this he managed to buy a second-hand microscope. On the advice of Sir Grimwood Mears (of whom more later), he also bought a copy of the Reverend A. E. Eaton's *Monograph*. This is a massive tome, the size of a family bible, containing hundreds of detailed drawings of river insects in the different stages of their life-cycle – larva, nymph, dun, and spinner.

He made a fly hatchery – a long narrow wooden box divided into a series of compartments each separated from its neighbour with fine perforated zinc through which a current of water from the river could pass from end to end. Now he was equipped to study entomology. I have one of his notebooks by me as I write, and this is a typical extract:

Centroptilum pennulatum*

Male Spinner. Upper eyes red-brown or deep orange, lower eyes mottled green blue or black. Upper eyes having an almost white band underneath dividing them from the

---

*One of the species of large pale wateries.

stem which is a bright yellow. Segment between the eyes and the thorax – namely the neck – dark red brown. Upper thorax light brown yellow. First segment of abdomen dark brown red or similar colour to the neck. In some lights the colour of the eyes is identical with the upper thorax but this colour is given to the upper eyes by the stem. Middle segments translucent white tinged with yellow. Last four segments deep brown red of similar colour to the first. Setae white almost silver, legs similar. Wings transparent, blue tinged.

Length of body 9 mm, wing span 18mm

Habits. Caught on 10 June 1946 while dancing near the river. Flies are difficult to catch as they dance high above the ground. Noticed perhaps fifty in an area of about an acre. Weather cold, stormy.

This is one example of many. Looking through his work, one cannot but be amazed at the painstaking care with which he observed, analysed, and recorded. With only the minimum of education, he taught himself to cope with the Latin terminology used by Eaton, and technical words such as 'integument' and 'thorax'. Encouraged by Sir Grimwood, he began to correspond with Martin E. Moseley, Director of Entomology at the British Museum (Natural History). Mosely, an eminent scientist and fly-fisherman, wrote to Sawyer in November 1943: 'I have examined the animalculae under my microscope and I see that your observations were more accurate than my own and I must withdraw my too hasty pronouncement that they were caddis larvae.' Here we have the leading authority on entomology in England apologising – and doing it generously – to a humble river-keeper.

Several of the nymphs which Sawyer sent up to the Natural History Museum were accepted as part of the permanent collection and are still there today, including nineteen examples of *Centroptilum pennulatum*.

◇   ◇   ◇

Frank Sawyer married in 1933 and in two years he was a widower, his wife dying of tuberculosis. In her final illness, she was nursed by her younger sister, Margaret Dunford. Margaret and Frank came together in the face of tragedy and married. In due course four children were born – Janette, Judith, Tim, and Pat. All now have families of their own.

They were a happy and united family. His children recall the stories – always, of course, about wildlife – that he told them. He had the joy of coaching his son Tim and seeing him develop into a first-class fisherman. They all enjoyed his company and their idea of a fine day out was to picnic on the downs with him. Many who knew him in later life did not appreciate his sense of fun, but his family saw it, and it is plain in the stories of his boyhood in Part One. Those like 'Duggie' Newell who joined him for weed-cutting say that he turned the drudgery into laughter.

Certainly he was happiest with his family and by the river, but he enjoyed shooting and was a first-class rifle and game shot. Committee meetings and visits to cities were things that he endured. He was proud that all his children passed the eleven-plus exam and went to grammar schools in Salisbury. Janette became a nurse at the Royal Victoria Hospital at Boscombe, Judith a secretary at the British High Commission in India, and Pat an accountancy assistant in local government. Tim works for the Forestry Commission and is at present Head Training Forester for the South-East of England.

◇　　◇　　◇

Sawyer's study of entomology, which fascinated him for its own sake, had a strictly practical purpose. This was to devise artificial nymphs, and ways of fishing them. When he became keeper in 1928, the Secretary of the SDFFA was Brigadier-General H. E. Carey, who later wrote a book, *One River*, about the upper Avon. Carey was an enthusiastic disciple of G. E. M. Skues. He discussed Skues's theories of fishing the nymph with Sawyer, and lent him some of Skues's patterns of nymphs. These were all tied with legs, and were intended to lie in the surface film. But Sawyer had already seen fish taking nymphs deeper in the water. He began to experiment with artificials that would sink. First he used lead, but that destroyed the appearance to the fish. He hit on the idea of using copper wire, which fulfilled two functions. It weighted the nymph and it replaced silk as a tying medium. It also glinted in a lifelike way. He developed first the pheasant tail nymph, and later the killer bug, the grey goose, and the bow-tie buzzer. Details of how to tie these nymphs, and how to fish them, are given later.

Sawyer gave some of his nymphs to Carey and explained his ideas. Carey tried them but was not impressed. One has the impression that he thought Sawyer something of an upstart. Who was this young keeper who thought he could improve on the ideas of the great Skues? So Sawyer worked quietly on, in the obscurity of a Wiltshire village, and it might have remained so had it not been for Sir Grimwood Mears, who deserves a section of this book to himself.

14

Sir Grimwood Mears

SAWYER joined the police reserve as a special constable during the thirties, and when war came in 1939 he was called up full-time into the police and stationed at Netheravon. In 1944, when his age-group became due, he was called up into the Royal Artillery and stationed nearby at Larkhill. He was released in 1946, having had a nervous breakdown. The regimented life of the services did not suit him at all. Strain and frustration took their toll of him, and he had later nervous breakdowns. No strings were pulled: it was pure luck that, for most of the war, he remained near the Avon.

So he was able, between 1939 and 1945, to keep an eye on the fishery and to work for it in his spare time. Fishing of a sort continued and one of those who spent much of his time by the river was a retired lawyer, at one time Chief Justice of Allahabad, Sir Grimwood Mears, KCIE. He was a widower, living at the Avon Hotel* at Amesbury, a small town about three miles downstream from Bulford.

---

*Now the Antrobus Arms.

What kind of man was Sir Grimwood? In the Introduction to *Nymphs and the Trout* (1970), Sawyer pays a glowing tribute to him: 'His faith in me gave me faith in myself and rather than let him think me a failure I did my best. So great was his influence over me that I have never written, indeed will never write, without seeing his image before me.'

It has not been difficult to find out what Sir Grimwood was like for a number of people in the villages and in the BBC in the late forties remember him well. He was clearly what is usually known as a 'character'. In appearance he was a large, burly man with a resemblance (from photographs) to the late Mr John Foster Dulles. He had old-world polished manners and a fruity, port-and-Stilton voice. In his time as a judge he had apparently had to sentence several men to death and there was certainly an iron hand beneath the velvet glove.

He met Sawyer from time to time by the riverside, as all members did, but took no particular notice of him until one day Sawyer mentioned that he was studying aquatic insects under a microscope. 'Where did you get a microscope from?' he asked. 'I bought a second-hand one,' replied Sawyer. From that moment, Sir Grimwood's full attention was roused: he realised what a sacrifice that must have entailed. He questioned Sawyer closely and soon knew that he was a man of most unusual talent and promise. He took Sawyer under his wing, making him his protégé, and launched him in two careers – one literary, and the other with the BBC.

Sir Grimwood knew many of the well-known figures in the piscatorial establishment of the day, among them G. E. M. Skues, then living out his old age at the Nadder Vale Hotel (which no longer exists) at Wilton near Salisbury. He arranged for Sawyer to visit Skues, and in the Introduction to *Nymphs and the Trout* Sawyer recalled the meeting:

This was in 1945. The memory of this first meeting is still very clear. Skues was then nearly 90 years old. To me he looked a little fragile old man who wore a black skull cap to cover his extreme baldness and heavy lensed glasses to aid his sight. But though frail in body and aged in appearance I quickly found that his brain was very alert and this became more and more apparent as our discussion developed.

103

Skues had been a solicitor and was trained to deal with matters far more complicated than fishing. His ability to sort out the corn from the chaff, so to speak, was brilliant, as was his questioning and grasp of the answers. I had tea with him on this first visit and we talked for more than two hours.

I watched as, with shaking hand, he took down notes from time to time in a minute and spidery hand which, good though my eyes were at that time, I found hard to read without the aid of magnification. I wondered then how he could have possibly constructed the beautiful little dry-flies he had in his boxes and the various nymph patterns he had evolved through the years.

In that same year, 1945, Skues wrote as follows:

Dear Mears,
   Of course I shall be glad to give Sawyer a letter of introduction to A. & C. Black but it occurs to me as likely to be more valuable if I wrote to them direct advising them to keep an eye on him as an angling writer of exceptional promise whom they owe it to themselves to catch.

                                             Yours, GEMS
Sorry my fist is so awful but it is so cold and I am past my first youth.

The correspondence between Skues and Sawyer continued right up to Skues's death in 1949. The subject was nearly always entomology, with Skues commenting on Sawyer's observations. But sometimes Skues allowed himself a glint of his old humour, for example: 'Mr Mosely was a great devotee of Mr Halford and got very shirty at any adverse comment.'

Skues introduced Sawyer to Mr H. D. Turing, then editor of the *Salmon & Trout* magazine (father of the distinguished writer, and later also editor of the same magazine, Miss Penelope Turing). Turing published Sawyer's first articles and Skues watched over them with a fatherly eye. No ignoble thoughts of a young upstart riverkeeper daring to disagree with him entered his head. Small and frail physically, Skues was a big man in every other way.

All these early articles were the product of a great deal of toil in Sir Grimwood's room at the Avon Hotel. Although Sawyer wanted to write, it did not come easily to him, and the lack of education was a severe handicap. But he persevered, taking the same infinite pains that he always took. Among his papers are some two hundred articles and radio scripts, and three books, Nowhere in all this have I found an ambiguity – something anyone who has tried to write good English knows is not easy.

By the early fifties, Sawyer was ready to write a book, and the result was *Keeper of the Stream* (1952). He had written a number of articles for *The Field*, and when he needed help in arranging and editing it was natural that the task should fall to Mr Wilson Stephens, then editor of *The Field*, who was a keen fisherman, a leading angling writer, and a highly professional journalist. Readers can judge for themselves what they think of *Keeper of the Stream* from the extracts which follow. It is, at present (1983) out of print, but second-hand copies fetch £20 and it seems likely to be reprinted soon.*

In 1958 Sawyer published the first version of *Nymphs and the Trout*. Wilson Stephens ensured that it was very readable, but compared with the 1970 version it was bare and the theories of what later became known as the Netheravon style were not fully developed. He later improved the dressing of his nymphs, and he mentions the killer bug, devised to kill grayling, in a rather apologetic way because it imitates a freshwater shrimp and could be said not to be true fly-fishing – it was justified because grayling were vermin. Later, he discovered that on still water the trout took it for a hatching sedge. He then ceased to be apologetic about it.

The 1970 version of *Nymph and the Trout* was virtually a new book. The theories were fully thought out, his experience in other parts of these islands and in Europe had broadened his mind, and he was now able to express himself on paper as a professional. Although writing was always something of a penance, if he felt deeply enough about something he could write memorably.

Nymphs and the Trout has since become a classic all over the world.

---

*Allen & Unwin plan to re-issue it in 1985.

For the last decade of his life, Sawyer wrote less. He had a regular column in the *Shooting Times* but he suffered from headaches and it became more and more of a strain. The last serious writing he did was to contribute a chapter to a book called *Masters of the Nymph* published in the USA by Doubleday in 1979.

So much for his literary career. Now we must return to the days just after the Second World War, when everyone listened to the wireless, and television – flickering, black and white, unreliable – was in its infancy.

◇   ◇   ◇

In 1950, the BBC published a booklet entitled *Broadcasting in the West*. It is full of names once well known, now only the faintest of memories. For instance, Ralph Wightman, A. G. Street, Brian Vesey-Fitzgerald, Ralph Whitlock – and one who was beginning an illustrious career, John Arlott. There is a picture of Sir Grimwood and Frank Sawyer by the river. Sawyer is in the lead carrying a rod and pointing out a fish. Immediately behind is the large, solid figure of Sir Grimwood, staring intently and holding one of the big, cumbersome microphones of those days. The caption reads: 'Sir Grimwood Mears, whose commentaries by the Wiltshire Avon have become radio classics. Here he is with the man who catches the fish, Frank Sawyer.'

Mrs Sawyer has kept a recording of one of those broadcasts, on a heavy 78-rpm disc which Tim Sawyer has transcribed on to a tape. Sawyer catches a fish at Bulford Mill cottage, just above the hatches, and when the fish – a heavy one – bolts through the hatches,* he strips off his line, ties a cork to it, lets it go down through the hatches, runs round to the pool below, casts out another line and hooks the first, ties it on again, and lands the fish. Sir Grimwood's fruity voice, boyish enthusiasm and effortless command of English make it as exciting to hear as the Grand National. I hope that the BBC may think it worth rebroadcasting.

All this began in the spring of 1946, when a young BBC producer called Peter Maggs was called into the office of the Head of Programmes at Bristol. 'We have heard', said the latter, 'from a man called Sir Grimwood Mears who says that the item

---

*See the map of the Bulford Bridge area on page 14.

we broadcast last week about trout fishing was rubbish. If we go down to the Avon, he says, he will put us right. Go down and make a recording – it might be worth three minutes on our weekly magazine programme.'

Peter Maggs duly went down to the Avon and met Sir Grimwood, with a gawky, shy Frank Sawyer lurking in the background. It was a lovely spring day full of birdsong, the mayfly was on the water and the fish were feeding hungrily. 'Set up your equipment, tell me when you are ready, and I will begin,' said Sir Grimwood. Maggs did as he was told and Sir Grimwood began to describe the scene. Then, when directed, Sawyer caught a fish. Within two minutes, Maggs knew that he had found a star. Sir Grimwood was a natural broadcaster.

This was the beginning of a number of broadcasts in which Sir Grimwood did a commentary while Sawyer caught a fish, studied the insects, or did one of his jobs as river keeper. The BBC crew enjoyed themselves by the river. Sir Grimwood would supply a picnic of Fortnum & Mason standard, and Maggs remembers him saying: 'Do try this. It is an *educated* Brie.' On another occasion he added (to Maggs's amusement), 'I would not be averse to the odd guinea.'

Gradually Sawyer's confidence grew and he began to play a bigger role, until he broadcast regularly on country matters from the studio. There are about fifty of his scripts in the BBC archives, mostly dating from the late forties and early fifties, either from Bristol or Birmingham. For a talk broadcast on 17 May 1951, Sawyer was paid four guineas plus 3rd-class return fare from Salisbury to Bristol (14s 7d). Well might he too have asked for 'the odd guinea'.

Sawyer had an attractive voice: the long, soft vowels of Wiltshire made it easy to hear and distinctive. It did his confidence good when he found that his country tones were actually an advantage. Peter Bale, another BBC producer, remembers how early on Sawyer was paralysed with 'mike fright'. So, indeed, are most people. But he was a perfectionist, went on, and re-recorded until it was right. When King George VI died in 1952, the BBC broadcast a programme of farewell and Sawyer was chosen as 'the voice of the west'.

What of Sir Grimwood? As Sawyer's star waxed, so his waned, but entirely without ill feeling on his part. He was delighted with Sawyer's success. He did a popular series of his own on radio in which he told stories of his years in India. He continued to fish on the Avon, and Sawyer was with him when he caught his last trout. He was well into his eighties when he died in 1963.

During the fifties, Sir Grimwood moved to Ipswich and Sawyer used to visit him there. The cost of such a journey would have been a considerable proportion of his earnings. It was evidence of his affection, and perhaps continuing need, for him.

In the early fifties, television was growing apace. The BBC still had a monopoly – ITV did not begin until 1954 – and there was a captive audience of about eight million. They were captive in the sense that their only option was to switch off. When the BBC decided to make country programmes, Sawyer, with his well-known voice, deep knowledge of the country, and craggy good looks, was an obvious candidate.

In the next chapter, he tells how he made one of the first of these programmes.

15

Fishing for Television

THROUGH the years many people asked me what is entailed in the making of angling programmes for television. Having done a number of these programmes I think I can give you the picture from both the technical and angling viewpoints. I must explain there are three different methods employed. One, and by far the easiest, is by filming. For this, a portable camera is used and pictures of this or of that are taken over a period which might be hours, days, weeks, or even years. The film is then cut and linked into some kind of sequence, and then a commentary is taped to synchronise. Background sounds, such as bird music, moving water, or rustling trees, are then added and the programme is ready for transmission.

A second method is to use both camera and sound-recording apparatus. Pictures, voice, and background sounds are all synchronised on the site. This, of course, needs a larger crew for operation but, again, it might be done in hours, days, or weeks.

The best parts of the film and commentary are 'cut', formed into sequence, and linked to run for the specified time of transmission. Often such programmes are done months before they are due to go on the screen. Complicated and worrying as these might be, they are the least difficult when compared with the third method, which is known as OB – outside broadcast. With this there can be no hours or days in which to get an actual programme, for it is transmitted direct from the scene of operation. The programme is billed to start at a certain time and finish at a certain time. It might be scheduled to run for twenty minutes, or for half an hour, and the success or otherwise of the show depends on what happens during that specified period.

I can speak with some experience of this method for I took part in the first BBC outside broadcast fishing programme and, I think, all others to date.* And so my explanation will be from a personal angle. Plans for the programme are made months in advance, and the date and time for transmission are booked. If we are lucky, as we have been on several occasions, we get a date and time which may give a fair chance for sport and for general interest. But once this is arranged there can be no alteration. Luck plays a big part, for who can tell when planning in January what conditions are going to be like at the end of May or in early June? So many things could be adverse. Until the moment transmission starts there is no peace of mind for anyone concerned, least of all for those who have to do the actual show.

First there is the collaboration with the producer and the booking of date and time. Then comes the choice of site. This is not as easy as it might appear. Your own idea of a good site for fishing and for general scenic effects may not suit the engineer's transmission, or be suitable for light or sound. It might be too difficult to get the OB equipment near enough, or to lay on telephone and electricity services. So this place, a favourite one, is ruled out. So, perhaps, is the second choice, and so on. Eventually, a site is selected which may suit everyone else but sadly reduces the chances of sport and of seeing wildlife. But you agree there is a chance, for you know of a fish or two in this locality, and from then on this is accepted. Perhaps they will be in the mood to show at the right time.

---

*Written in 1968.

The trouble is that you haven't taken into consideration that the OB equipment will be several big vans, lorries, generators and various private cars, and that a sixty- or eighty-foot mast has to be erected close by. Neither had you realised that there will be a team of men and women totalling between twenty and thirty who will be working near to the fishing site and wandering along the river banks for a fortnight before your programme is due. You did not know that a camera was to be mounted on a platform over the river, just where you had marked down a good-sized trout. Nor did you know there would be a second camera, which would run on a wooden platform beside the river bank, or that a third would have a position on the opposite bank. It is explained that certain cables must run across the river bed and there will be things you must try not to trip over. Could we have that branch of a tree cut off and that bed of weeds trimmed? And so it goes on until all is finalised. The meadow beside the river has the appearance of a fairground. All is set, but now we must check the positions and sound. This is on the day before the programme is due. Everyone then to his appointed place and a run-through is organised.

By now perhaps you can understand the state of mind of the man whose job it is to catch a fish and to run a commentary. All the wildlife in the locality has had the wits scared out of it and there is no sign of a fish. However, you go through the motions, a check here, a check there, for positions, and all is well, apparently. Then to your further dismay you learn there will be a complete rehearsal in the morning. You are wanted at a certain time and must do exactly as intended during the actual programme. When this is finished everyone will be kept away from the river until the programme is due.

The following morning I am rigged up with a radio microphone with the various wires and batteries stowed away out of sight in convenient pockets of my fishing jacket. For this I have a special attendant whose job it is to make sure all is rigged properly and to switch on the batteries at the right time. I am admonished to be careful not to scrape the microphone with my rod, net or tackle bag, and to be careful when bending in case a plug should pull free. Along comes the producer. He would like me to go through the actions of fishing, but there's no need to catch a fish. Just as though the river was full of trout waiting for me to cast a fly! No, no need to catch a fish, but he would like me to mime the netting of a trout and showing it to the camera. I must hold the fish in my hands.

'I'll show you with this piece of stick! Then walk to camera No. 2 and stop about six feet away. Hold the fish steady. You can make a mark where you wish to stop, if you like. Run your commentary if you want to, but it does not matter what you say, as long as you say enough to get the sound effects right. If you wish to speak directly to the camera, then remember this must be No. 1.'

With briefing done, all is ready for rehearsal. The producer retires to the scanner where he can see the pictures from all three cameras on his monitors. There he is linked by headphones to the stage manager who is now in sole charge of the outside operations.

I stand by waiting for his signal to start the rehearsal. With my mind whirling with a thousand thoughts I watch for the fall of a hand. Down it goes. All the responsibility of the show is now mine and I feel very much alone.

I must confess I hate these rehearsals but realise they are necessary. On I go from action to action, from place to place, trying to remember this and that and avoiding the maze of cables as best I can. I realise I am chattering a lot of nonsense as I do the make-believe. I can't wave a hand or press a button to start the flies hatching or get a general movement of the wildlife around me. It is these I have to rely on, for the wild creatures are the actual stars in this kind of programme, but you cannot tell them when to perform. Still I go on through the whole procedures and at last the rehearsal is over.

A further discussion with the producer takes place. There is a little correction of a position or an act and all is set. I insist then that everyone is kept clear of the river banks, which is agreed, and then I am offered some coffee. But I want none of this. All I wish to do is to go somewhere quiet and get my thoughts straightened out. And so I wander off to a seat beside the river and sit there alone. My inside is all of a flutter, my head aches with conflicting thoughts and I would love to lie down and sleep. I watch the river, and, as if to try and still the turmoil in my head, a mayfly hatches, and then another. I then realise that it is a most beautiful day, warm and sunny. Sparrows and chaffinches appear as though from nowhere and so also do swifts, swallows and martins. A fish rises with a splash, another shows behind a weed bed. More mayflies flutter across the river. In a moment my brain has cleared and my tiredness vanishes. My performers are on time and we might be lucky after all.

Time moves on faster, but as flies appear and are taken either by bird or by fish I begin to get impatient. I feel the best chance to get a trout will be gone before we can start. I welcome the call to get ready.

With one eye on the river and deaf to all the people around me, I am rigged once again with my microphone and the batteries are switched on. Suddenly it is quiet, so quiet that I can now hear the ticking of my watch as the second hand creeps on towards the minute. Then comes the signal. Transmission has commenced. Now I am alone once more and, regardless of what may happen, the sequence must go as planned or there will be confusion. Though a fish might rise close by, I cannot yet cast for it because the preliminaries must first be done. I have to describe the locality, talk about the river, about insects, birds and animals and a lot more. My fishing can only take place at the appointed time.

All the while the producer is ringing the changes with his three cameras, showing a wide shot of this or a close-up of that. But I am quite happy. I have no thought of anything save the nature in my view or what I can hear. My wild friends have come to my aid, to perform as I had hoped so much they would. The time passes on quickly. My fishing tackle is all ready and now I can try to catch a fish. As I chatter, I note a good trout rising eagerly to take mayflies some thirty paces upstream and near my bank. Here I feel sure is a good chance and, taking my usual precaution in approach, I creep along to get within easy reach. But a noise behind me attracts my attention and there, trundling along on its wooden track, is camera No. 3 and its two operators. I see a bow wave as my trout goes headlong for the nearest cover and I have to wait and watch for another. Fortunately a good hatch of mayflies has come on. A second fish moves in midstream and then, in the tail of my eye, I see that a crowd of villagers have wandered down the opposite bank right into the focus of the camera covering my actions.

While I am deliberating another trout rises under my bank, an easy one to reach, and, without moving from my position, I drop my artificial over him and up he comes. As my rod flicks back so I feel the check as the hook takes hold and I have the thrill of a fighting fish. It is an anxious time. Will the hook hold, or will the fish escape before I can get him to the landing-net? As I draw the trout into the net and lift him clear to the bank I heave a sigh of relief. No need now to mime. This is the real thing, and it is with a feeling of excitement that I show the trout to camera No. 2 and at the same time do my best to talk intelligently.

My mind is then at rest and no longer am I at a loss for words. As I continue to fish and run my commentary I glance at my watch and know the signal to conclude the show must soon come. But there is still time to get another trout and just then a fine fish shows twice in succession a few yards upstream. As I move along to get within reach he rises a third time, but, even as I lengthen line to make my first cast, I get the signal that my time is up.

The river and the surrounds are gently faded out as the announcer brings the programme to its conclusion: 'That was Frank Sawyer fishing for trout on the Wiltshire Avon.'

NOTE

That was written in 1968. In television today, it would be unthinkable to do such a programme live, and to risk total disaster. As Sawyer writes, his wild friends came to his aid – but no one can give them orders. The modern use of video cameras and light, portable sound equipment has made it comparatively easy to record and edit.

There was another reason for the 'OB'. Television was a brand-new medium, competing against the cinema, which then had a mass audience. Most of the population went to the cinema once or twice a week. The early television people wanted to exploit television's main advantage over the cinema – its ability to show events as they happened. And it can be said that what programmes like Sawyer's lacked in an artistic sense (as against an edited programme) they made up for in immediacy.

Sawyer did about a dozen television programmes for the BBC during the 1950s and 1960s. The first few made the most impact. These were some of the first nature programmes ever broadcast on television. The mass audience saw a man's way of life beside the Avon – a man in tune with his environment, who did not spend his life in an office, who did not queue for buses, walk pavements or breathe fumes. It seemed to them idyllic. It awoke something deep and primeval in those millions of suburban hearts.

sv

— 16 —

Keeper of the Stream

Rescued from the Flood

IT DISTRESSES ME to see the flooding of a valley for with it sometimes comes tragedy, not so much perhaps for the aquatic creatures which live in the river and streams but for the thousand others which are part of the valley life. I think sudden flooding is a thing for which nature did not prepare all her family, and a quick rising and overflowing of the river finds some of them at a disadvantage. A few years ago a cloudburst sent a wall of water racing down the valley to the sea – a wall which, as it advanced, spread far out on either side of the river course, to cover all but the highest parts of the low-lying meadows.

I went down the valley that day and the tragedy I saw I shall never forget. Though I tried, I was powerless to help to avert it. It all happened so suddenly. Water swept over the river banks of reach after reach, and flowed out across the meadows like a tidal wave. As the vegetation of the valley was covered, so the surface of the water became alive with panic-stricken, struggling creatures. Moles, shrews and fieldmice swam side by side, moving from one dry patch of land to another amidst hordes of insects of many descriptions that were milling about and drowning. Field-voles and water-voles came bobbing up from their sodden nests in search of refuge. Some clambered up trees, some scrambled on to driftwood or other flotsam, and were swept away down the valley – poor, shivering little animals whose homes were left and lost for ever.

At one place the centre part of a footbridge rose above the swirling waters, and though a hundred yards away I could see movements of life upon it. I walked through water nearly to the tops of my waders, and then could see what they were. Two water-voles dived as I got nearer and swam to a nearby tree, but huddled together on the wooden bridge were three moles, seven fieldmice and two little pigmy shrews, all with their fur sodden, and shivering as much with fright as with cold.

I had a sack with me, and none of the little animals made a move to escape as I took them by their tails and dropped them into it. I turned them all loose amongst the tufts of grass on the high ground and in a moment all had disappeared. The three moles bored into the ground as though their lives depended on their getting beneath the surface. Perhaps they did. I have heard experts say that a mole cannot live more than a few minutes without food. I had much proof that they can. Perhaps these three were more hardy than some, for I learned afterwards that a friend of mine had seen them on the bridge an hour earlier, and he thought the pigmy shrews were two of their babies.

Moles were my chief interest that day. At one place, I could see the ground heaving at several points on a small mound about the size of a kitchen table. It was sixty yards away from me, and the water surrounding it was too deep for me to wade. As the water rose I could see the movements gradually concentrating towards the centre, then first one, then another, and finally four little black bodies appeared on the short grass. Panic-stricken they ran here and there, to stop and turn at the edges of the water, and then the first made up its mind to swim.

People say moles are short-sighted: perhaps they are. Some say they are blind, but it seems to me that nature has provided them with an uncanny sense of direction. Each of these moles swam to where I was standing on the high ground and which was for them the only place of safety. All were exhausted as they landed but, with scarcely a pause each bored down into the ground and, with the soil moving above their heaving shoulders, began tunneling towards still higher land.

The Philosopher

Many of my conversations beside the river illustrate the hold that fishing has on a man, no matter what his cares and responsibilities. A chance encounter with an army officer proved a case in point. His face, though aged and lined with worry, was familiar and as my thoughts raced back through the years I remembered his name.

'Captain —— ——,' I started to say, then stopped at the look of amusement he gave me. 'No, no, Sawyer,' he hastened to say, 'not now. I've been promoted since I last saw you. I am a major-general.'

I apologised and then congratulated him. I felt pleased that with his rise in rank and fortune he had not forgotten his fishing days of long ago – there he was, just as excited about his prospects of catching a trout as he had been then, when duty and trouble weighed lightly upon him. I did not waste time in asking questions. I thought he wanted to fish and enjoy his day on the river. Trout were already moving, time enough later on to talk of the intervening years. So, putting him on to a brace of rising fish, I left him.

The general, when greeting me, had said, 'You haven't changed much, Sawyer.' Well, perhaps not, in face or figure. But as I wandered downstream I knew I had altered considerably in other ways. Even as he had risen in his profession, I felt I had risen in mine, for I had learned much in fifteen years. But how different were our two lives. His had been a study of peacetime military organisation, and then of war: mine had been a study of nature, and to find how I could help to create and to foster. I began to wonder which of us was the more content. . . .

All around was the music of birds, the deep mellow tones of the blackbirds mingling with the songs of the warblers. Bees buzzed around the blossoms and river flies danced in the rays of the sun. Occasionally the surface of the river was broken and as the rings made by a rising fish spread gently towards the banks, all else could be forgotten by the fisherman.

All else could be forgotten. Was it to catch fish that the general had come to the river, or was it for another purpose? I came upon him later that day. Without his knowledge, I studied him. There he was, crouched low behind a fringe of willow herb with rod in hand. His eyes fixed intently for a few moments on a spot under the opposite bank, then they would sweep upstream and down, watching the activities of the swifts and swallows, then to rest a while on a vole busily munching a strand of weed on a tree-root, on to a wagtail flitting about a weedbed to take the hatching duns. And he was listening to the young starlings calling to their parents from amid the blossoms on the hawthorn bushes.

Occasionally he would glance to the artificial he held in his hand, and always his glance would return to that spot under the other bank. Though I could see his actions and his interests, I could not read his thoughts. But as he turned in my direction the expression on his face was enough. No longer was it the face of a commander of men – it was the face of a boy, enraptured. No thoughts of war or destruction could bring that peaceful repose. He was content and happy. I discreetly withdrew.

It was evening when I saw him again, and he was preparing to leave. 'Sawyer,' he said 'I have enjoyed my day, but how differently from what I expected. I came here this morning to be quiet, so that I could have a chance to think over an important paper I have to write, but today this stream and valley have been far removed from war. My report is still unfinished, I have not attempted anything and, for the first time in months, I feel refreshed. What is it about a river that makes you forget?'

Well, there was no need for him to ask that question. He should have known, even as I did. That day he had been near to nature, he had been seeing and hearing some of the things he was meant to see and hear, and they had communicated a feeling of peace and happiness to his tired brain.

The Sunken Nymph

Nymphs and nymphing trout can be put into two categories – the active and the hatching. I believe that the active nymph is in the stage in which it is most likely to be taken by trout, and the active nymph is within a day or less of hatching into a dun. It is the perfectly mature insect in a stage when it is anxiously waiting for conditions which will enable it to complete its life-cycle.

Though I call them active nymphs, perhaps restive nymphs would be a more fitting term to use. Their underwater life is over, no food is required or taken, they are just waiting until they feel that weather and water conditions will be satisfactory for them to mate, and for the females to return to the river to lay their eggs. And so, many of the mature nymphs come out from their shelters where they have lived in security from the fish, to move about the river. Some climb up the vegetation to cling and crawl about on the fronds just beneath the water. Others delight in swimming from one weedbed to another, and still more move freely about in mid-water, swimming towards the surface and returning to the gravel of the bottom once more. Most of them will wait until the cool of approaching evening, or possibly until it is dark, before they decide it is time they left their liquid home for ever.

Throughout the day this restless movement of nymphs will continue and who should know more of their habits than the trout? Indeed they do know of them, and so station themselves in places where, without much trouble or exertion, the nymphs can be intercepted and eaten. Often enough, the best position for a trout to see and catch these active nymphs is near the river bed, for there he can obtain an unrestricted view of his surroundings. Unless something very attractive passes above him on the surface he is quite content to take only the insects which move in the small area around him, an area which often enough does not exceed an 18–inch radius. There he may lie throughout the day and unless some big fly, fluttering and gyrating, passes above him on the water, he will not rise to the surface to give an indication that he is feeding.

It is useless to try to tempt such a fish with an artificial nymph fished just below the surface, or to cast a dry fly over him. He is expecting his prey to be moving near to the river bed and if he is to be deceived and caught the presentation of the artificial must be made in a natural manner. It is necessary to get the nymph down and into his radius of vision and so the artificial must be constructed accordingly. The trout's view of a swimming nymph is to see the insect with its legs tucked in close to its body, and with these active nymphs the wing cases are a very conspicuous part. So in tying a representation these two features should be considered. Hackles to suggest legs are unnecessary but the body should be built so that the thorax is accentuated. It should be remembered that the nymph has to sink rapidly through the water. I find it pays to dispense entirely with tying silk and to use, instead, a very fine copper wire of a colour which merges with the general tone of the tying. With this fine wire I build up the body and thorax to make a base for the dressing and to give additional weight to the hook. In fishing the representation, the finer the cast, within reason, the better.

NOTE

Sawyer goes on to explain that the second category – the hatching nymph – had already been fully covered in the writings of G. E. M. Skues. This is the nymph in the last few moments of its life, struggling to hatch through the surface film.

Sawyer elaborated and developed these ideas in *Nymphs and the Trout* (1970), but what is given above is the basic theory.

SV

121

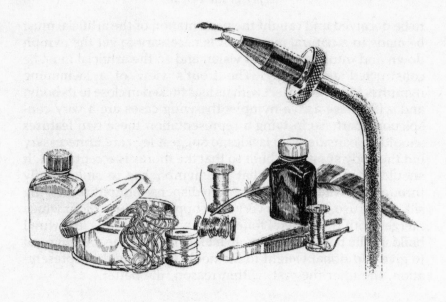

17

How to Tie the
Sawyer Nymphs

The Pheasant Tail Nymph*

Now AS to the dressings. The materials used are quite easy
for most who are interested to obtain. To represent the several
olive nymphs, my pattern of the pheasant tail can be constructed
on hook sizes 14, 15, or 16, and I make no claim that the use of
pheasant tail fibres for a body of nymphs or flies is original. But
what I do claim is the manner of base building, ballasting, and
the tying in of the pheasant tail fibres with fine copper wire, of a
colouring to suit and tone in with the general dressing. Artificial

---

*This was called by Oliver Kite 'one of the most effective patterns ever devised by man'.

nymphs tied in my way are not difficult to make, and the simple instructions I am able to give should be sufficient for anyone with nimble fingers to follow.

First grip the selected hook firmly in the vice and then give the hook an even covering from bend to eye with fine red-coloured copper wire. The wire we use is little thicker than a human hair and this one can obtain at little cost from various sources. It is used in the windings in small transformers, dynamos, or electric motors. After the hook has been covered and the wire locked so that it cannot spin round the hook shank, wind the wire in even turns to the point where the thorax of the nymph is to be constructed, and there build up a hump. Then wind the wire back to the hook bend and let it dangle. Wire is much easier to use than silk as it will not spin off or loosen if the tension is relaxed.

The wire with its red colour forms the base for the dressing and at the same time gives additional weight to the hook. I dispense entirely with the use of silk and use the fine wire to tie in the dressing. The wire is now dangling from the hook bend. Take four centre fibres from a browny-red cock pheasant tail feather. Hold the fibres by their tips and then tie them on with the wire so that the fine ends stand out about one eighth of an inch from the hook bend. They form the tails or setae of the nymph. Then spin the four fibres of the pheasant tail on to the wire so that they are reinforced, and then lap fibres and wire evenly to the hook eye. Hold the wire firmly, separate the fibres from it and then wind the wire to the point behind which the thorax is to be made. Bend the fibres back and fasten for the first lap of the thorax, then forward to the hook eye again. Fasten here securely with half a dozen turns of wire and then cut away spare fibres.

Our finished effort should have a very pronounced thorax which suggests the bulging wing cases, and a body which tapers neatly to the tail. With the tail fibres spread, all is complete.

It will be noted by those who follow these instructions that the upper part of the thorax which imitates the wing cases, is much darker than the rest of the body. This is brought about by the lapping back and forth of the butt ends of the pheasant tail fibres. If wire and fibres are wound evenly on the hook, the spare ends should have the dark tone which is a feature in the butts of these fibres. This gives a very natural appearance to the thorax. The fibres of pheasant tail vary in length, and indeed texture, from the butt of the feather to the tip, so when dressing a nymph one can select lengths most suitable for the size of the hook, bearing in mind that when the body is made the dark part is ready to use for lapping.

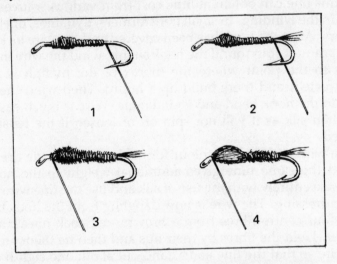

Diagram of the Pheasant Tail Nymph stage by stage.

When wet this pattern has a translucent effect and one can see the red of the wire showing through the pheasant tail fibres. The artificial, so constructed, has a very good entry to water and will sink deeply when required. The hook point is not muffled or guarded in any way by hackles or by the dressing, and a slight lift of the rod will drive it home.

The Grey Goose

My second pattern represents the pale wateries. This also is of simple construction and should be made in three different sizes, as suggested for the pheasant tail – Nos 14, 15, and 16. I use fine copper wire in the construction of all my nymphs but use different colours according to the demand. For the base of this pattern, the grey goose, I use a golden coloured wire and also this same colour for tying in the dressing. For the tails, and the body and thorax, I use herls from the wing feather of the ordinary farmyard grey goose. Only a few of these wing feathers are suitable and only the parts of these which have a lightish, grey, green, yellowish appearance. The construction is somewhat similar to the pheasant tail. Take out four herls from the wing feather, tie these in so that the tips can form the setae for the nymph, and then dress in the same manner as with the pheasant tail. At the butt end of the herls the colouring is darker, as with the pheasant tail fibres, and this, lapped backwards and forwards, can bring about a well defined thorax and wing cases. As with the first artificial, the colour of the wire is one of the features. The gold shows through the dressing and is very marked at the head end.

NOTE

At Two Lakes on 30 September 1976 – the last day of the season – not a fish had been caught by noon. Because the season was ending, there had been no stocking for some time and the fish were educated. But they were showing on the surface, so I tried a grey goose nymph and took a fish of 2 lb 12 oz. I lent one to another angler and he took a fish, and then I lent one to Admiral Sir Geoffrey Norman, who took a fish of over 7lb. Where normally fifty or sixty fish are taken, these three were the only fish caught all day.

SV

The Grayling or Killer Bug

I now come to the dressing of what has come to be known as the killer bug. This, as I have mentioned elsewhere, was a name given to it by an American friend. I devised this originally to kill grayling in the upper Avon but in later years found it to be very effective when fished for trout in reservoirs and lakes. Also in a much larger version for salmon and sea trout.

Once again this is of very simple construction, so simple indeed that anyone looking at it could be forgiven for thinking it could not possibly deceive a fish. These we construct in sizes varying according to the requirements, from Nos 12, 11, and 10 to 9 for lake and sea trout. Generally, however, it is the smaller sizes which are in greatest demand.

To make this bug, grip the hook firmly in the vice and then give the hook a double covering, wound evenly, of wire – colour of this not important, but normally we use red – which can be much heavier than that used in the construction of the nymphs. When the double covering has been done leave the wire dangling at the hook bend. Then start at the eye end of the hook and lap in securely a length of wool. The colour and texture of this is important. I call it wool, but actually it is a mixture of wool and nylon, produced and carded for mending purposes. The manufacturers of this product give their name as Chadwicks and they list the colour as being 477. Actually it is a natural and not very easy to obtain. However, this is by the way.

After locking in the end of the wool, give an even winding to the hook bend, back to the eye, and then once more to the hook bend, so that in fact the base is covered with a triple layer. Then, holding the wool tightly, use the wire to tie it in securely at the hook bend with about four turns. Then cut off both wire and wool neatly.

NOTE

The wool which Sawyer recommended, Chadwick 477, is no longer obtainable, and Coats Paton, the manufacturers, have no record of the dyes used in making it. What is required is a rough grey wool with a pinkish tinge. Many substitutes have been tried and all catch fish, but some are better than others, and probably none is as good as Chadwick 477. Mrs Sawyer has a good substitute which she uses on her nymphs.

One card of Chadwick 477 has enough wool on it (about 5 yards) to last one fisherman a lifetime. It is astonishing how many chalk-stream fishermen still have a card or two and jealously guard it. I know at least one who intends to make a special provision in his will for his.

These three nymphs, as well as the bow-tie buzzer (whose dressing is described above), are still tied by Frank Sawyer's family and can be obtained from Mrs M. Sawyer, 325 Lower Street, Haxton, Netheravon, near Salisbury, Wilts SP4 9PU

SV

18

Fishing the Sawyer Way

The Netheravon Style by Charles Ritz

ON 10 JULY 1952, I arrived at Netheravon, on the Avon, to watch Frank Sawyer fish. He is a big man with red hair and in his fifties, sympathetic, modest and realistic. He has been keeper of the Officers' Fishing Association water since 1928.

The water is several miles long and the river full of trout and grayling. It was two o'clock in the afternoon and we decided to go the river at once.

When we came to a reach of calm water with a depth of approximately four and a half feet, I noticed rises, small rings, regular and spaced out. I was under the impression that they were rises after midges. Sawyer began getting out his line and said that the rings indicated that the fish were taking nymphs beneath the surface. He cast upstream and placed his nymph about six feet from the selected ring. The nymph sank at once. Visibility was good and we could follow easily the floating part of the leader, which grew shorter during the drift. Sawyer explained to me that you must watch the leader at the point of immersion for that is where the smallest reaction will become manifest when a fish touches the nymph. Suddenly he very slightly raised the point of his rod, a movement followed immediately by a delicate strike and he had taken it. I had not clearly understood what he was about, but, having landed a fine trout, he said:

'When I thought that my nymph had passed the fish without being taken I slightly tightened my line *to give animation to the lure*, which often incites a fish to take.'

We went on to the next. This time I was able to see clearly a sudden acceleration in the sinking of the leader followed by a strike, and a grayling of a pound and a half was taken. The third and the fourth fish were victims of the same tactics, but I must admit that once again I was able to see nothing. The last time, according to Sawyer, the sudden sinking of the leader was imperceptible, but there had been a slowing down in its drift.

Some of the fish he caught were taking nymphs almost on the surface (visible rings) as the nymphs were trying to break the surface to hatch, but others were in different stages of evolution. The rings reveal the presence and approximate position of the fish. In general, fish that are not near the surface lie at a depth corresponding to that of the water. It is therefore desirable that the artificial nymph should sink very deep to reach the fish. To attain precision, you must know the speed of the current and the rapidity with which the lure will sink so as to determine the point at which it should penetrate the surface to ensure its passing close to the fish. The speed of the current is a fixed factor; that of the sinking of the nymph can be regulated (by a change of nymph), as can the place where the lure enters the water. The taking of a fish is indicated by a change in the movement or speed of the drift and the submergence of the leader.

After about an hour's fishing, my instructor had caught eight fish and missed two. This excellent average was due not only to his great mastery but to the fact that he knew the conditions by heart.

When my turn came, my eyes were already tired and the light was slightly less favourable, though still good. How should I make out? I am always inclined to strike nervously. In the result, I took two grayling out of five, thanks to the assistance of my instructor. By the end of the lesson I was astonished to find how much assurance I had already gained. I thought of the grayling in Austria. What splendid times were in prospect!

'Now we shall fish by sight,' said Sawyer. 'I've kept it till the last for it is undoubtedly the most exciting method and requires the most rapid reflexes.'

We went downstream. It was not long before we saw a fine trout, lying in a pocket with a sandy bottom, in the process of feeding on nymphs. Sawyer showed me how the fish fed with sudden, rapid movements towards an invisible prey, the appearing of the belly. At last, I began to be able to note it a little for myself: slight movements of the head and tail, the appearance of the inside of the mouth. The master took three fine trout and then made me try. I failed miserably with the first two. Too late each time! Finally, the third, moving to take my nymph before it arrived within reach, gave me the necessary warning. We could not see the cast and therefore our only mark was the movement of the fish. This, in my opinion, is what matters most, but – there is always a sixth sense!

Striking in this kind of fishing requires the most sensitive of reflexes. Casting must be very accurate: the same technique as for the dry fly but combined with calculations as to the speed of sinking so as to obtain the drift which will present the nymph correctly. The fish very quickly grows wary. Therefore the first presentation is very important.

Sawyer decided to try another locality: 'Let's go over to that big tree by the little artificial dam I built of concrete blocks. We'll find a colony of grayling and trout there. It's an ideal observation post. The light there makes it possible to see the fish's slightest movement.'

When we got to the spot, having walked well away from the bank to avoid any possibility of alarming the fish, we hid behind the trunk of the tree, from where I was in a position to observe a unique sight: some twenty fish, among them several fine trout, were grouped together and ceaselessly taking nymphs. There were three grayling near the bank and Frank took them one after the other without failure. But how quick his reactions were! I was able to see only the last take his nymph. Then he took two trout, one of which weighed two pounds. And he did all this without alarming the fish, thanks to his first presentations being as accurate as if he were fishing with a dry fly. He immediately took the fish downstream and landed them there.

I was now beginning to see the grayling take the insects, and then I saw a big trout do so. My eye was at last becoming acclimatised, and I caught a grayling. The fish rose slightly at the moment of striking. Then, six or seven yards away, I saw a fine trout. I presented with precision and suddenly saw the white of its mouth. I struck too late! I tried again several times, but it was no good, the trout had become wary. I tried two others. I saw nothing of the first but a streak of lightning. The second moved quickly and slightly to the right. I struck. I had him! Sawyer was delighted. Then there was a period of calm. The fish seemed no longer to take the slightest interest in my artificial nymphs. Nevertheless, Frank, in order to prove his mastery, succeeded, after a short delay, in taking my big trout, though he admitted that he had not seen the actual taking of the nymph and had succeeded only thanks to his sixth sense.

I was amazed at the intense activity of the fish during a period of taking nymphs and by the astonishing possibilities of this kind of fishing. I shall never forget that afternoon, my excitement and the satisfaction of having discovered and learned something really new in the practice of fishing. I am eternally grateful to Sawyer, who revealed his secrets to me with joy and enthusiasm.

That evening, in an inn at Amesbury, Sawyer explained the whole technique of fishing with a nymph, and here is his explanation:

In the first place, the conditions must be suitable: nymphs, larvae and fish must be active. The water should be rather low and the light favourable. On English chalk streams it is better to wait till July.

Sawyer has spent more than twenty years observing the life of aquatic insects, particularly under the water and at depth. He has studied them in their daily life from the egg and the larva to the stage of the nymph. He has succeeded in watching their underwater movements, as they go from one weedbed to another, how they fold their legs along their bodies and use their tail as a means of propulsion, thereby obtaining the maximum of ease and speed in swimming.

Skues seems to have concentrated his observations mainly on the activity of flies immediately preceding the hatch, therefore when close to the surface. That is why his patterns of nymphs have their legs detached from their bodies, which hinders their sinking.

Sawyer maintains that when the olives are on the move the fish do not expect to see a nymph swimming with its legs dragging behind its head. The suppression of these hackles gives the artificial nymph a better outline and facilitates its presentation beneath the surface. It sinks in a more lifelike way, Sawyer thinks that Skues fished close to the surface, at the stage of the nymph's inertia, while he fishes more often than not at some depth and even very deep.

The colonies of nymphs swim about like little fish, rising occasionally towards the surface, then diving for about a foot before sinking finally to the bottom. This may be repeated several times before the hatch. During the last two weeks of their existence, these insects move over a great area of the bottom, journeying from place to place, from one shelter or patch of weed to another. When you see a trout posted between two lots of weed, you can watch all the movements of the nymphs.

What I like about Sawyer is that he refuses to allow himself to be hypnotised by theories of overprecision. He is always in search of the simple, the practical and the essential and attaches importance above all to the *method of presentation* (the type of leader, the weighting of the artificial nymph and the exploitation of the various possible stages in the development of the insects). And, rod in hand, he can prove that he is right. For him, the nymph is a microscopic submarine which must respond immediately to the slightest command transmitted to it by his rod. And, in the last resort, he says that with practice and patience one ultimately develops the blind man's sixth sense of anticipation, the height of mastery.

I hope that this account, rather long perhaps, but in my view indispensable, will allow those interested in the nymph to benefit by the indisputable advantages of this method of fishing, which every good fly-fisherman ought to try, having first furnished himself with the types of nymph recommended by Sawyer.

As far as I am concerned, it is the acme of the art of fly-fishing.

Nymphing in Stillwater

The art of nymph-fishing in lakes and reservoirs is becoming more and more popular and I foresee the time approaching when the old and well-tried method of fishing a team of wet flies will be abandoned in favour of the single nymph on a leader tapered to a fine point. A light, well-greased or non-sinking line, with rod and reel to suit it, will make up the outfit. Only in recent years have I come to know and really enjoy the sport there is to be had in fishing the still waters. I must confess that previously I thought that the catching of trout in lakes and reservoirs was a poor substitute for river fishing.

How wrong I was, and how mistaken are those who still hold such views! However, much of what I learned about nymph-fishing in rivers for trout and grayling has helped me considerably when adopting a similar technique in the stillwaters. My fascination for this kind of fishing was clinched for me when I spent a fortnight in the mountain lakes of northern Sweden. There I had plenty of time at my disposal to work out theory into practice. So when I fished again in the lakes of this country I was able to go at it with quite a different approach and with success fresh in mind.

My wife cannot understand why I like to visit Chew Valley, to travel a distance of sixty miles and then pay a pound* to fish when trout are plentiful in the water I look after and in other parts within easy reach. From her point of view perhaps it is rather amazing, for no doubt there are many who fish at Chew Valley and other reservoirs and lakes who would love the chances I have to fish rivers.

I would not go to any of the lakes if I had to fish a cast of wet flies or monstrous lures which need a heavy line and a powerful rod to cast them. It was only after I found by much perseverance that it is possible to get good sport with light tackle and a single

*Written in 1961.

nymph, or lure, that I began to class it as exciting and interesting. Trout in lakes will take small nymphs and lures quite as confidently as those in the running stream. But the whole secret of success lies in the ability of the fisherman to place the nymph where it can be seen by a fish, and in such a way that the fish is deceived into thinking it is a natural creature.

With lake fishing I have come to the conclusion that it is nothing but a waste of time to cast indiscriminately and search an area of water unless one or more fish have shown themselves at the surface. Even then there is little reward if these fish are not moving regularly. By this I mean a rise form here and there at intervals in the water which can be covered. To catch lake fish with nymphs the trout must be feeding in the upper foot or so of water, indeed not below the depth to which the nymph or lure will sink, and where it can be given the required movement.

The important thing is to know that there are fish within reach. In rivers it is possible, in most cases, to see fish and, even if they are not to be seen, if one rises you know he is likely to be still in the same position. What is more, in the running stream you know very well in which direction the head is pointing and therefore can deliver the nymph accordingly.

In the lakes the trout continue to move, to search in fact, and in so doing will travel about over a very large area. But their search is a thorough one and to me it seems very possible that each fish selects a certain beat and keeps to it for a while. On various occasions I have found that if I note the area of a rise form and continue to cast to that spot the same fish can be caught there even though he has many acres of water around him.

At times it might mean casting to that one place for ten minutes, or even longer, but eventually patience is rewarded. One can only imagine what these lake fish are doing. To me it seems possible that they cruise on a long beat which might take them along the shore for a considerable distance, or perhaps the beat takes them out towards the centre of the lake. At some point they reach a territory worked by other fish and so the return is made.

The big trout at Chew Valley are no longer the easy fish they were during the first two seasons this lake was opened for public fishing. At the time, as in many other stocked reservoirs newly opened, the fish would take almost any lure or wet fly which showed some sign of life as it was dragged through the water. Many, of course, had to forfeit their lives as a result but others escaped with an education which I feel sure has been communicated to other fish now living in the water. I don't think it is wise to underrate the reasoning powers of fish, or for that matter any wild creature, and though it may sound silly to say they can warn one another of danger I feel they can advise each other as to what is good to eat.

And so today it is necessary to use artificials which very closely resemble, in shape, coloration and movement, the kind of animals on which trout feed when they rise to the surface. As in rivers, the fish have a large variety to choose from and the stomach of a trout can contain up to a score or more of different creatures. But there are some animals they like much better than others and when these are seen they are taken regardless of whether it is just an isolated appearance or not.

On an early visit to Chew Valley, a friend and I caught fish with a lure I devised many years ago to take grayling in the chalk streams. I thought then that the lake trout took this because they thought it was a hatching sedge, the rising pupae of the brown silverhorn, and now I feel very confident that I was right. Since that time I have been to Chew Valley on different occasions throughout the season and each time I have fished with confidence, a confidence I inspired in the friends who went with me. We all caught fish. I knew we would as we were offering the trout a representation of one of the creatures they see and take frequently.

The grayling lure* does indeed delude the lake trout into thinking it is a hatching sedge. But the general shape and coloration is not enough. These lures must be fished correctly or much of the attraction is lost. I found this to be true when fishing them to grayling. Occasional fish will take the lure as it sinks but the majority are attracted when a movement is imparted to the lure by the fisherman.

This movement is not a haphazard one. It should be made in a cool and calculated way when imagination must play a big part. First you must know a little of what the trout expects to see. With the hatching sedge this is the insect coming up through the

---

*This is the killer bug, whose dressing is described on p. 125.

water to hatch. It is seldom that these come up vertically and often they will swim along just beneath the surface for a few yards before emergence, looking for a place to cling, such as a weed stem on which they can crawl to the air and then hatch. A study of these creatures among the weed banks around the margins of lakes can give one a good idea of their habits. Compared with the nymphs of the ephemeroptera, the speed of movement is sluggish. They have a slow and rather laboured effort made on an even plane – a movement which can very easily be simulated by a fisherman using his rod in the right way. . . .

First, as I have already written, find a place where fish are showing. Use a quick-action rod with a light line and a leader tapered to a point fine enough to allow quick sinking of the artificial. Grease the line well and also the butt of leader. Cast the lure to the area where a fish has shown. Continue to cast if necessary but each time watch the floating line and leader butt. Watch to the point where the leader enters and disappears beneath the water.

These instructions will possibly bore those who already know and adopt the technique. But each day others are keen to learn anything which might help them towards some sport. For these I must write with some clarity. The heavy lure sinks quickly. Pause a moment or two after casting, a period calculated to allow the artificial to sink about two feet. Then, with rod pointing low over the water, gather in all slack line until a drag commences. Then slowly lift the rod tip whilst continuing to gather in line. Sometimes the take of a fish is felt and a quick flick of rod tip will set the hook, but more often the take is indicated by a draw on the floating leader butt or line – a kind of reverse of the arrow-head which shows as the free line moves towards one as it is being gathered in. Quick action with rod tip is then essential but this is not as difficult as it might at first appear. In lifting the rod to impart a drag, the rod comes into a very easy position, in fact it is already flexing with the pull of the line so that instant contact can be made by a flick of the wrist.

In this kind of fishing it is necessary to use fine points. The finer the point, the quicker the lure will sink and the more attractive it will appear beneath the surface. The fine point allows more wobble or action of the artificial. With the fine point it is essential to have a light line and rod, a rod with a sensitive tip which will flex to the wrist action needed in hooking. Some may say that you cannot hope to land the big fish of Chew Valley with light tackle. With this I strongly disagree. (The authorities at Chew recommend a minimum point strength of 7 lb. — S.V.)

But different tactics must be adopted. The moment a big fish is hooked he should be allowed to run if he so wishes. Just hit him, hold the rod up so that it flexes to the pull and let the reel run. A hundred yards of 10 lb breaking strain nylon does not take up much room on a reel. If a fish wants to run that distance then let him. It is doubtful if he will. Usually he pulls off about fifty to eighty yards and then the drag of the long line slows him up. When he stops, a quick recovery of line can be made, and it is very unusual for a second and longer run to be made. If the hook has been driven home when the fish takes it will continue to hold. The light tackle means one has to be careful and the playing out of a fish may take a little longer before it can be brought to net.

When fishing at Chew I use the same rod and line I use for the more delicate fishing of nymphs in the chalk streams; indeed, excepting for a slightly stronger leader point, the outfit is identical. With this I get great enjoyment, and at the end of a day a feeling of satisfaction that I have treated the lake fish with the same respect I show to the wild trout in our rivers.

A New Idea for the Buzzer

Most stillwater fishermen, I feel sure, will agree with me when I say that of all the aquatic creatures which excite trout into rising the buzzers have been the most frustrating to represent, both in the construction of an artificial and in the successful fishing of it. Many and varied are the patterns I have seen and tried and many are those I have evolved myself which I thought would give me confidence when fishing, but to no avail. This went on until about four years ago* when I put into practice an idea that had been in my mind for a long time. It is with pleasure and with a certain satisfaction that I pass the idea on to those who may be interested in giving it a trial.

*Written in 1970.

We have named this pattern 'the bow-tie buzzer'. This was a name suggested for it by an old friend who had tried it with success in the West Country and it is a name which I think will be remembered. I had made enough different patterns of buzzers to know that it was not just a good copy of the natural that was required. I knew too that when these creatures were hatching it was almost useless to try to interest fish in representation of anything else. The fish got their eye in, in a manner of speaking, and looked for that one something they expected to see. Shape and general coloration was not enough.

The trouble was that the deception could not be helped by a movement of rod and line, as is the case with the majority of nymphs and other representations of creatures which swim, or make a horizontal movement through the water. Buzzer nymphs cannot swim in this sense; their movement to or from the surface is mostly in a vertical plane, upwards and downwards, not through the water. They have no real legs or setae to act as propulsion units. The manner of ascent or descent is by a series of loops or convulsions, a wriggle more than any straightforward swimming.

Because of this and because also these nymphs have a habit of hanging in mid-water and at the surface, I found it extremely difficult to incorporate anything in the tying which could simulate movement, the kind of movement a fish expects to see.

Then it occurred to me to try a nymph in two parts. One of the main features of the buzzer is the white fringe, or celia, present at the front of the head. This shows very prominently when the nymphs are about to hatch and is in continuous movement. And I felt, if I made this separately, and so that it could have free movement in the water, that I would accomplish something worthwhile. Then it struck me that this could be carried on the end of the leader. A little bow-tie, in fact, which could move in the eye of the hook. At the same time I accomplished something else for, with this attachment, the nymph could hang almost vertically in the water and, if so desired, the body could be made to spin around the leader.

So now the secret, if indeed it is a secret, is out. All you have to do is to make up a nymph body of a size, shape and coloration to suit the natural, and then make up the bow at the end of the leader at the time you want to fish.

However, making up the body is no simple matter if it is to look similar to a natural about to hatch which, of course, is the time when the fish go mad to take. At this time the whole appearance of the creature changes from a dull, almost drab effect to one that is translucent, almost luminous. The whole body has a sheen of silver along it which makes it show up very plainly in the water. This seems to shine through the integument almost like a light and brings out the main colours. The silvery appearance is accentuated as the shuck of the insect is being thrust clear of the body and in my tying I have tried to incorporate this effect. The partially slipped shuck is represented by body fibres draping the hook bend. The accompanying drawings show the sequence of construction and the manner of making the bow-tie in the leader. All that is needed is a description of the materials. The wire used is gold-coloured, over which is lapped a strip of silver foil (1, 2 and 3). This acts for the base. Then tie in four fibres of browny-red cock pheasant tail. Tie the fine ends so these can act as the slipping shuck, then dress over the silver foil so that the sheen from it can show through (4 and 5). Build up the head end to a hump and finish off the tying behind the eye (5).

The bow tie can be fashioned from a piece of white nylon wool. The hook size most suitable is No. 12. The down eye is preferable. Thread end of leader upwards through hook eye of nymph, then disregard it. Fashion a slip knot (6) at the end of leader and pull this tightly on to the piece of wool. Trim with sharp scissors to make the little bow (7). Care should be taken not to make the bow too big. Afterwards the nymph can be slid up to the bow and all is ready to start fishing (8). If tied correctly the bow cannot be pulled through the hook eye. The weight of the nymph holds it in position while casting and a slight tightening of the line after a cast has been made will ensure the bow is in the right position. Hanging as it does on the leader makes no difference in the hooking of fish; indeed, such a position usually gives a very secure hold.

I have used the tying in many different waters and have had great success and sport with it. I have found no difficulty in making the bow tie; indeed the tying of a slip knot and trimming of the bow takes no longer than attaching a leader in the ordinary way. I hope my experience will be yours also.

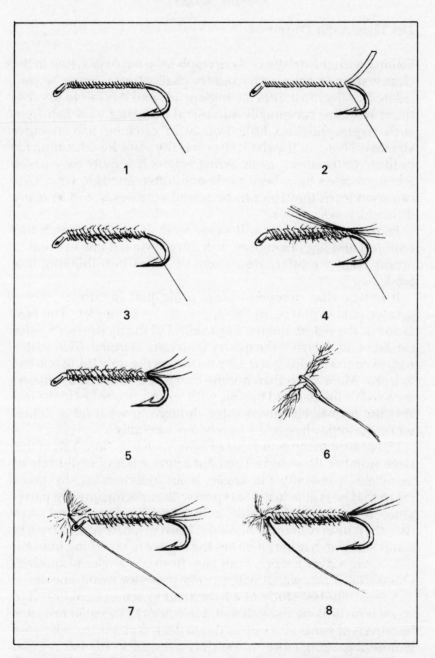

Diagram showing the tying of the Bow-tie Buzzer stage by stage.

Frank Sawyer

The Fisherman Observed

Fishing with the dry fly or the nymph for trout or grayling in the clear waters of our South Country chalk streams must be considered as the most difficult angling art, and it is fair to say that those who are continually successful in taking wild fish from such rivers will find little trouble in catching fish in other streams. There on the chalk stream is the place for education for in these transparent, meandering waters it is quite easy to see when mistakes have been made and, often enough, why. One can soon learn that fish can be scared very easily and in many different ways.

Frightened creatures will never feed. If one is to catch fish with rod and line, then these fish must be in a frame of mind to accept what we offer, after being deceived into thinking it is food.

It is true that deception plays a big part in success, but a greater part is played in the approach by an angler. The best tackle in the world and the most skilful of the fly dresser's wiles can be of little avail if the quarry is already alarmed. Skill with a rod, of course, helps but it is by no means the only thing one has to learn. More often than not the difference between the fisherman with a full bag and the one with an empty one lies in the fact that the former has given some thought to what he is doing, while the other has acted purely mechanically.

I have seen many hundreds of fishermen in action. Yet, of this large number there have been but a few whom I could rate as first-class. Generally the angler is an individualist. By this I mean that he is able to get his sport without being one of a party. Once he has learned to throw a fly, or pitch a nymph and catch fish, then he is content to be alone. Least of all, he has no wish to stand and watch others if he has the chance to be fishing himself. But, being a river keeper, I can pass from one angler to another. Often, too, I can watch without my presence being known.

A few minutes' study of a fisherman in action is all I need to know if he is likely to catch fish. He whom I can see in full view hundreds of yards away up or down the river bank, he who goes blundering along close to the river dressed in his full regalia, with his rod pointing to the sky and flashing in the sunlight, will say, 'Your trout are much too shy for me to tempt them.' Then he will ask. 'Do you think I might do better farther up, or down?' as the case might be.

One has to be diplomatic and yet it is only for the good if the truth is told. It is for the good of others, too, when many rods have to fish a short stretch of river. Not that our stretch is a short one. It extends for over six miles. Yet I have known some of our members to cover the whole of the fishery in a day and still not have a fish at the end of their journey. In this journey they may have put down scores of good fish they have not even seen, and, in so doing, made conditions far more difficult for others.

But there are those who have learned by experience. There is the man who is in no hurry. The stretch of a couple of hundred yards of water will keep him occupied until he wants to go home. If fish are moving to natural food, he has noted the position of every one within his range of sight, and will be dealing with them as he thinks fitting.

I did not at first see this angler, because he was concealed. But a movement caught my eyes. His head appears slowly from behind a clump of willow-herb, then I see his rod as it catches the light on the varnish. Movements to and fro follow as the line is lengthened and then cast. The rod bends suddenly and stays in an arc and there is a disturbance in the water. But that is all. Some moments pass and a flurry of water at the river edge. The head moves slightly forward as a landing-net pokes out from the willow-herb to dip into the river. The rod arches back with the butt held vertical. I see the net lifted clear with the gleam of a fish at the bottom. Then all is quiet again.

A few minutes pass and I see the head appear over the top of the willow-herb once more. Then a creeping form moves along the river bank, low down, almost as though on hands and knees. Then it merges into more of the riverside foliage and from my sight. I know that he needs no advice from me.

Nymphing in Sweden

A knowledge of aquatic insects can be a great help in bringing sport to a fisherman. It can, in fact, make all the difference between having a full and an empty bag. Through the years I have studied most of the creatures in the chalk streams of the South Country, and now, whenever I visit other rivers or lakes, I make a point of finding out as much as I can about the life in them. Recently* I visited a string of most beautiful lakes, high in the mountains of northern Sweden, near to the borders of Norway and Lapland and close to the Arctic Circle. Here, at this high latitude and altitude, I came across an insect genus which was completely new to me, but which appeared in such numbers as to form the main attraction for the large brown trout in these waters.

The Swedish fishermen are interested in nymph-fishing and wondered if the technique would be successful in some of their mountain waters. I decided to try it. I have used it in many places both in this country and abroad, and as in each case I have been successful with one or other of three patterns of artificial, on hooks no larger than No. 14, I confidently included a number of each of these with my equipment. But although I caught my first two fish on a No. 14 pattern I found I had to revise my opinions considerably before getting any real success.

It was the spinners of the strange genus which I saw first, the imagos, and I thought they must be ephemeropterans allied to the March brown, as their size and colour were not dissimilar. These spinners came to the lakes in large numbers to lay their eggs by dipping on to the water where rapid streams entered the lakes down rock-strewn courses. Here, above the bubbling and well aerated water the spinners gathered in thousands. As they mated and eggs were laid, so both sexes fell spent to the water and drifted gradually out on to the lakes, and as they drifted so would the trout rise.

But though I persevered with my various nymphs, and then tried dry flies, both large and small, I had no response. It was the same when I tried wet flies. Not a rise did I get, yet the trout continued to take these spinners from the surface. So thick were the flies that the fish were taking one and missing several before taking the next. Obviously no representation of the spinner, no matter how well constructed, could compete with the naturals. Yet I felt sure these fish could be caught.

I decided, before doing any more fishing, to study these strange insects. In this I was lucky. I found the nymphs and watched some as they transformed to duns, and then I knew

---

* 1959.

that this was no relation of the March brown. The nymph is streamlined and so constructed that it can swim through water like a little fish. The dun is a handsome creature with a body not unlike that of a freshly hatched mayfly. But with wings which are darker but in colour close to those of the blue-winged olive. Indeed, on the water, with the wings slanting back over the body, these duns looked very much like giant blue-winged olives. However, I knew they were no relation to *ephemerella*. The appearance of the nymphs proved that.

The more I studied them, the more I was convinced that this was a genus completely new to me. I collected specimens of nymphs, duns and spinners, but it was not until I returned home that I was able to identify them. I am fortunate in having a copy of Eaton's *Monograph*, and in this I found a good description of the genus and some beautiful and detailed drawings of the nymph and nymph parts. Finally, I sent specimens to Mr D. E. Kimmins at the British Museum. The insects are of the genus *Siphlonurus* and my specimens were *S. spinosus*. They inhabit waters at high altitude and are not known in this country. There is, however, a good mention of them in Harris's *An Angler's Entomology*, where they are referred to as the summer mayfly.

But the nymphs are not like others of the swimming group with which I am so familiar. Though they can move through water faster than any I know, the habit of transformation from nymph to dun is more in keeping with that of our flat, crawling group, such as the March brown and yellow may dun, that of creeping up to the surface on rocks, banks and vegetation and there clinging at the surface while the nymphal shuck is cast. Few hatch in open water, and these apparently, are at a great disadvantage when trying to do so. I found the nymphs were distributed fairly evenly all about the lakes, but as hatching time drew near so they migrated to the outsides or to where rocks or vegetation enabled them to crawl to the surface. Afterwards the duns would take flight to shelter in the forest on the mountainsides where the changes from dun to spinner took place.

The trout in the lakes had little opportunity to take the duns except on days when a breeze carried freshly hatched insects out on to open water. These duns appeared to have some difficulty in making a take-off from anything other than a substantial perch. The migration of the nymphs to the lakesides took place mostly in the mornings up to midday, but the hatching of flies was during the afternoons. Spinners came to the water to mate and for egg-laying at late afternoon and early evening, from about four o'clock to sunset at about nine o'clock. The egg-laying was a brief procedure.

I cannot say what life-cycle these creatures have but I think it cannot be more than a year, as I found none in larval stage. I would say that the eggs hatch quickly and that much of the growth is made within a few weeks. This, however, is conjecture based on the fact that little food can be available for such creatures before midsummer.

To find that these *Siphlonurus* have nymphs of the swimming group interested me considerably, and the study I made of them gave me every reason to think that an artificial constructed and fished to represent them in the water would be effective. So it proved. Fortunately, I had taken with me some fly-tying equipment, including some wing feathers of an ordinary domestic grey goose. The nymphs are large and I found they could be fashioned best on a No. 12 or No. 11 hook. A base was built up with fine red-coloured copper wire and then four fibres from the grey goose wing feather formed the tails, the body and the wing cases.*

This artificial, which I christened the SS nymph, proved most effective. I used it during the nymph migration period in the mornings, while duns were hatching in the afternoons, and when the spinners were thick on the water in the evenings. With it I connected with more than 60 trout and landed 44. Many of these weighed more than two pounds, and my best brace were four-pounders, but I was broken by others much larger. It may be thought that these fish in the mountains were easy prey. They were not. Far from it. The water was pure, cold and

---

*In *Nymphs and the Trout* (1970), Sawyer clarified the construction of this nymph. 'Originally it was called a grey goose, but I have no wish to confuse it with the one evolved to represent the pale wateries. It is true that the basic dressing of the SS is of herls from the grey goose wing feathers, but these are of a much darker shade, of those, actually which come from the primary wing feathers. The grey goose herls are from the secondaries. The construction of this is much the same as with the grey goose, the difference being that a dark-red wire is used instead of gold. In sizes 14 and 13 this pattern is taken very readily when the claret dun is appearing on the stillwaters.'

The SS nymph is still popular in Sweden.

perfectly clear, and the sky at this altitude gave the fish the opportunity to see with absolute clarity.

My tackle was an 8 ft 5 in., 5¼ oz split-cane rod with a 3¼ in. reel, a No. 2 double-tapered silk line and a nylon cast tapered to 3x. The technique of nymph-fishing calls for light tackle and a rod with a fast-action tip. I had it, and it dealt with these really wild trout to best advantage. Trout of two pounds would take out eighty yards of line and backing with one strong run, and one of the four-pounders did not stop pulling until more than a hundred yards of line were gone.

Few places in the world can be more beautiful than this setting in the mountains of north Sweden, more than 200 miles from Stockholm, beyond Grovelsjon. It is a place where few Englishmen have ever fished. Others may go there in the future and I am sure they will be welcomed by the Swedish fishermen, as I was, and enjoy the sport and the sights I had and saw and will never forget. If they do I hope they can share the satisfaction at finding that nymph-fishing can be the most fascinating and productive method of fishing for the fine mountain trout.

19

Relationships

Charles Ritz

IT IS DIFFICULT to imagine two men more different than Charles Ritz and Frank Sawyer. The gap between the famous hotel in the Place Vendôme, Paris, and a cottage in Netheravon, Wiltshire, might be thought unbridgeable: yet they bridged it and had a close friendship lasting a quarter of a century, based on the one interest they had in common – fishing.

From Ritz's account of his first day on the river with Sawyer it is clear that he greatly admired him. He was impressed with Sawyer's skill, and delighted with the charm and delicacy of his style of nymph-fishing. But, more even than this, I think he was attracted by Sawyer's life-style.

I am not suggesting that Ritz would willingly have given up the life of the Ritz Hotel or the wealth which enabled him to indulge his passion for fishing around the world. But fishing with Sawyer was a taste of Arcadia.

Ritz was a dapper little man with a zest for life. He had many interests, usually with a mechanical bent. For instance, he had a room at the Ritz fitted up with one of those elaborate model railways with tunnels, viaducts and turntables. He played with it for hours and was always designing new features. He had a long life, stayed fit until his mid-eighties, and packed more sheer fun into it than anyone I can think of. He certainly indulged himself as regards fishing, but he was generous and thoughtful.

He stayed a weekend with the Sawyers at Netheravon in 1974, travelling from Heathrow by train and bus and carrying his rods and luggage. One morning he came into the kitchen and gave Mrs Sawyer a resounding kiss. Turning to Sawyer he said, 'I did that because I felt like it.' Sawyer could never have encountered this Gallic behaviour before.

Ritz wrote after the weekend referring to Mrs Sawyer as 'Madame Escoffier'. It was a graceful compliment, for Escoffier was the great chef whom Ritz's father, César Ritz, had brought from Paris when he opened the Ritz Hotel in London in 1905.

Until he met Ritz, Sawyer had only one rod, given him in the early years of their marriage by Margaret. Ritz provided him with many rods and had a special 'Sawyer' rod manufactured for nymph-fishing. Typically, Sawyer gave his old rod to his life-long friend and occasional assistant, Harold Sturgess, who is now dead.

Sawyer developed his whole style of nymph-fishing with this old rod, which was not built for the purpose. Tim Sawyer describes it as 'slow in the action and even slower in the hooking. To catch a fish on a nymph one had to be extremely fast in the strike. It developed the reflexes to such an extent that the strike often anticipated the take of a grayling which was moving in the direction of the nymph.'

Every year Sawyer went to the Ritz Hotel in Paris, to a meeting of the Fario Club. This was a club of leading fishermen from many countries, entirely organised and financed by Ritz. The members met for a weekend of social events, to talk fishing, and to try out rods on a lake called 'the pool of pigeons' in the Bois de Boulogne.

Sawyer was proud of his membership of the Fario Club and enjoyed the weekend as long as it was concerned with fishing. But social chit-chat with grand dukes in a salon of the Ritz was not his scene; on these occasions he would sit quietly with a cup of tea away from the throng, where sometimes Dermot Wilson would join him.

Sawyer had a genuine affection for Ritz, otherwise he would not have invited him to Netheravon. And it must have been reciprocated, otherwise Ritz would not have accepted.

Sawyer admired Ritz's skill as a caster and rod designer. Ritz had beautiful split-cane rods made in France to his specification, and never missed an opportunity to publicise them. It amused Sawyer, and many others, that a man so wealthy should bother to sell these rods. But Ritz was always a businessman – which Sawyer, of course, never was.

Sawyer was well aware that Ritz was no naturalist, and had no more than a superficial knowledge of entomology. Ritz, on the other hand, knew Sawyer to be a true countryman whose life-style close to nature gave him a contentment that he, Ritz, for all his wealth, could never have.

The long relationship which gave such pleasure to both, and through them to so many others, is an outstanding example of the bond that fishing creates between people otherwise totally dissimilar.

Alex Behrendt

One day in the early seventies, I was fishing with Frank Sawyer at Two Lakes. 'There's a fish on the feed,' he said, and indicated a spot about twenty yards away. I stared hard at the dark, green water. Was that the flicker of a tail? I was not sure and in any case doubted the accuracy of my casting at that range. 'You try, Frank,' I said. With effortless rhythm he cast and the pheasant tail nymph fell softly. There was a slight pause, a lift of the rod tip, and at once a commotion in the water. A minute or so later he had landed a two-pound rainbow trout.

It was this incident that brought home to me the gulf that exists between the top-class professional like Sawyer, and the average angler. His ability to see into the water was astonishing, and he could drop his nymph at twenty yards to the inch. This was why he used to smile a trifle condescendingly when I suggested a day at Two Lakes. It really was too easy for him, but he liked to come and talk to Alex Behrendt, whom he respected as a good professional like himself.

Alex Behrendt was one of the first to start a small lake put-and-take trout fishery, in 1948 at Romsey, Hampshire. Now there are over sixty in Hampshire alone, but Two Lakes remains pre-eminent. Sawyer was well aware that Alex Behrendt did an outstandingly good job, and that Two Lakes was a business whose purpose, like any other business, was to provide a reasonable living for its owner. In his heart of hearts, Sawyer did not approve of put-and-take. To him, it was not fishing. And he thought that all fisheries ought to be non-profit-making clubs and associations, like the SDFFA. So his feelings towards Alex Behrendt were a mixture of liking, respect, and disapproval. Knowing this, I was always fascinated to hear them together. Alex Behrendt, a fair and straightforward man himself, saw the same qualities in Sawyer. The respect between them, as professionals, was mutual. If Behrendt thought Sawyer's views on put-and-take fisheries old fashioned and out of date, he was too tactful to say so. My hopes of a good set-to between them were never fulfilled. They were both too well mannered.

Oliver Kite

Oliver Kite bought a cottage in Netheravon in 1958. His front door and the Sawyers' front door practically faced each other across the village street. For the first few years, they were good friends. Kite took Sawyer to fish at Two Lakes – one of his favourite venues. He spent many evenings in Sawyer's study learning about nymph-fishing and the entomology on which it was based.

But at some time in the mid-sixties there was an estrangement. They scarcely spoke, which given the situation in Netheravon must have been awkward to say the least. In local fishing circles, people still take sides – something I have no intention of doing. Whether there was jealousy, or whether the one simply made use of the other, is pointless to discuss and would merely be the raking over of old embers with pain to those still alive.

They were very different men, and what is of interest here is to compare them and so bring out some of the characteristics of both.

Olly Kite was good company by the river, a fine angler and a first-class instructor. He was a natural extrovert – a good mixer. He learnt quickly and wrote well. In 1963 he published a book on nymph-fishing in which he says of Sawyer that 'in a sense the whole book is a tribute to him'. Soon after this, he began a regular weekly programme on wildlife on Southern Television. These fifteen-minute programmes were immensely popular. They were on all aspects of wildlife, with the emphasis on fishing. In one, he stood in the middle of the Avon, a black hood covering his head, fishing with a bare hook for grayling and catching fish after fish. If he knows the location of the shoal and uses the 'induced take', any competent fly-fisherman could do it. There was an element of show business, but Kite was being paid to entertain the mass audience and this he certainly did.

Kite had an attractive and unusual accent deriving from his youth in Monmouthshire. It added to the pleasure of his performance. He took to television like a duck to water, his fertile brain forever producing new tricks to make the programmes more enjoyable. He was a media man, a born showman, with none of Sawyer's inhibitions or natural reserve. But he was not an original thinker. He had not the inclination, or possibly the capacity, for the long and painstaking research which is necessary before new ground is broken. This capacity Sawyer had in full measure.

At the height of his success, Kite acquired a white Jaguar of which he was extremely proud. His financial progress had provided him with a status symbol, and in this he was behaving just as the normal run of humanity behaves. Why not? He had earned it, he had the right to buy a green, red, or puce Jaguar if he wanted. But Sawyer would never have done this. He was not interested in status symbols.

That is not to say that money was not important to him: for most of his life it was a struggle to provide his family with the basic necessities. He was no businessman and never earned as much as he ought to have done. But he thought it wrong to make large amounts of money from fishing: it sullied the nobility of the sport. Money to Sawyer was a symbol of recognition of his standing. To pay him like a farm labourer was a kind of insult and hurt him deeply.

Both these men, who in their different ways gave so much pleasure to so many, died by the river, mercifully and with dignity. Oliver Kite had his final heart attack by the Test at Overton, Hampshire, on 15 June 1968. The story of Sawyer's death will be told later, in its proper place.

Howard Marshall

Howard Marshall was the first BBC sports commentator to become a household name. In the thirties, when Australia defeated England in a Test Match – which they often did – the whole nation was plunged into gloom and the voice which related these dire tidings as they happened was that of Howard Marshall. Car radios had not been invented and portables were cumbersome, so people mostly heard him in their living-rooms, ears glued to the loudspeaker. He had a pet phrase – 'over goes his arm' – and during those summers any comedian at a concert party on the pier had only to say the words in an exaggerated upper-class accent to be sure of a laugh.

Marshall and John Snagge could be seen every day at half past twelve, it was said, walking the corridors of Broadcasting House with measured tread on their regular visit to a local hostelry. During the war, Marshall was a war reporter; then he wrote for the *Daily Telegraph* and became co-founder of the magazine *Trout and Salmon*.

He lived beside the river Lambourn on the Berkshire Downs and journeyed one day to the Avon to fish with Frank Sawyer. He gave an account of the day in his delightful book, a fishing classic, *Reflections on a River* (Witherby, 1967). Compared with Ritz's bubbling, continental, enthusiasm, Marshall tends to English understatement; but the same note of wholehearted admiration is there, and some acute observation. He noticed how strong were Sawyer's wrists and forearms and how beautifully he used the roll-cast, 'flicking the fly easily across the river, with trees solid behind him'. Sawyer, he wrote, 'talked easily and naturally with an almost biblical simplicity and choice of phrase'.

Sawyer only talked like this with someone he trusted, so he

must have taken to Marshall, who could be said to have stood for everything good about the Establishment. He was urbane, cultured, polished, convivial and witty without being self-important or pompous. He must have been a splendid companion by the river or at a dinner table. Sawyer later spoke of him with affection.

In the flyleaf of the copy of his book which he presented to Sawyer, he wrote: 'To Frank Sawyer – great fisherman and naturalist. From Howard Marshall. 3rd November 1967.'

Wally Reed

Wally Reed, now middle aged, lives at Figheldean. In his youth he was not averse to a little poaching – as this tale, told in his own words, shows.

'When I was thirteen and sitting by the river at Figheldean, a trout was coming up for fly. I decided to take a shot with the catapult. I was lucky and killed the fish. I was using half inch lead ball – I had made it myself in a mould. The news went round the school, but not many believed it. Frank also heard of it.

About eighteen months later I was by the river when Frank came up. I had worked out by then the angle, the depth of water, the length of elastic, how to get the fish out, and had become pretty good at it. Unfortunately, the only time when weather and place were right, was during the fishing season. So I watched out for Frank.

On this day, when he came up, he said: 'Wally, you got that catapult in your pocket.'

'Yes.'

'You do get a fish with it, then.'

'I get one about every two weeks which I eat myself.'

'You know I will catch you one day.'

'Frank, you been after me these eighteen year. If you caught me, who would believe you?'

He burst out laughing. 'You would be right too. Cheerio.' And off he went.'

◇   ◇   ◇

Sawyer never forgot his own youthful escapades, and always had a certain sympathy for such as Wally Reed. But he would never tolerate anything blatant or excessive. Today, children are allowed to fish in the millponds at Figheldean and Netheravon – a wise decision. The irresistable urge which some children have to fish is given an outlet.

$$— 20 —$$

The River Keeper –
How the Avon Was Revived

The Great Cleaning

ONE RECENT* EVENING, having nothing much to occupy my time, it occurred to me that it would be interesting to work out some figures concerning trout population and production in the six miles of the upper Avon, in Wiltshire, which are in my charge. The outcome was surprising.

In 1930 we adopted a fry-stocking policy on the water, and the fishery depended on this method for its annual stock of trout. We started this fry-stocking when it was discovered that there

---

*Written in 1957.

was little regeneration from the wild fish. Indeed, the natural trout production was so poor that some provision had to be made to ensure sport in the future. I carried out considerable research at that time and continued to do so in the years which followed. Time and again I proved that practically all the efforts of the trout to reproduce themselves in nature were wasted.

There were seasons when I estimated that 1,000 pairs of fish spawned and yet not more than 1 per cent of the eggs hatched. In terms of ova and hatched fish this meant that of a million ova shed (allowing 1,000 for each hen) only 200 produced fish that survived the four years it takes for a trout to become of sporting size. My calculations were as follows: that of the 10,000 alevins produced, 50 per cent were lost by the time the early-fry stage was reached; that of the balance of 5,000 fry, 75 per cent were lost by the time the yearling stage was reached; that of the balance of 1,250 yearlings, 50 per cent were lost; that of 625 fish surviving as two-year-olds, 50 per cent were lost; and that of the 312 surviving as three-year-olds, 33 per cent were lost, giving a balance of 208 four-year-olds.

That may seem surprising, but it will be seen that the greatest loss occurred while the eggs were still in the redds. Actually the eggs were fertilised, the mortality occurring after the first three weeks of incubation. I arrived at the figure of 99 per cent loss after thoroughly examining many redds in different parts of the fishery, and came to the conclusion that the cause was lack of oxygen. The losses afterwards, though high, are not so important, as will be seen later. The fact is that, had we been obliged to rely on naturally bred fish for sport, we would have been very lucky to get more than 100 per season – from six miles of water – so we were obliged to resort to artificial means. The post-fry losses were due, of course, mainly to predators.

The comparative calculations for hatchery-bred fish – figures based on recent observations – are as follows: of 100,000 ova, 95 per cent hatched; of 95,000 alevins, 5 per cent were lost; of 90,250 fry, none was lost during its early stages, but 75 per cent were lost in the fry to yearling stages; of 22,562 yearlings, 50 per cent were lost; of 11,281 two-year-olds, 20 per cent were lost; and of 9,024 three-year-olds, 10 per cent were lost, giving a final stock of 8,118 four-year-olds.

These figures are, of course, only approximate, but they are, as I have said, based on recent observations. The losses through predators are plainly much less now than when I made my first calculations, but the total of more than 8,000 four-year-old trout from 100,000 eggs proves that previous heavy losses were due to bad hatching. Now the hatch is 95 per cent, and losses which follow still leave a respectable total.

But that total, though it is a lot of trout, is insignificant when compared with what could happen if nature had her chance. When river conditions are satisfactory, the natural hatch could be at least 90 per cent. In that case, assuming as before that the eggs shed by 1,000 female trout total a million, our calculations would show that 900,000 fry would hatch; 50 per cent would be lost in the alevin/early-fry stages; of the 450,000 fry surviving, 75 per cent would be lost by the time the yearling stage was reached; of 112,500 yearlings, 50 per cent would be lost; of 56,250 two-year-olds, 20 per cent would be lost; and of 45,000 three-year-olds, 10 per cent would be lost. So the actual production of four-year-old trout reaches to the remarkable figure of 40,500.

These calculations are sufficient to prove conclusively that the real answer to trout production lies not in artificial hatching and fry-stocking, but in making the river do the work as intended by nature. That such a thing can happen has been proved here on the Avon. My calculations are based on facts. Now, instead of the 1 per cent hatch we had from 1930 to 1953, we are getting at least 90 per cent. The time has come when there is no need for us to use the hatchery to maintain a stock of trout.

This successful hatching is due to the work we have carried out during the past three years. It has proved beyond question that the answer to the problem of natural trout production lies in having a clean and porous river bed, thus providing conditions whereby the eggs can have a continuous and plentiful supply of oxygen. In the past three years our six miles of the Avon have had a complete change. In many respects the river bed is now quite different from what it was. And the new environment has been accepted and approved by the trout.

The importance of an oxygenated water supply to trout eggs has yet to be understood fully. Indeed, I feel it is the solution to a problem which has puzzled me, and no doubt many others, for a considerable time. Hitherto I had thought that trout eggs received their aerated water supplies through the action of the running stream. By this I mean that oxygen was forced into the stream bed by pressure exerted by the various currents. I had assumed that the reason trout cut holes and throw up heaps of gravel was to ensure an anchorage for their eggs and to create a baffle which would cause currents to be driven to the bottom of the redd. Now I have good reason to think otherwise. My recent observations have proved that where trout eggs hatch successfully the water supply to the redd comes not from above but from below.

When trout make holes in a redd, they do so not with any idea of providing a nest and an anchorage, but simply because they want to cut through the hard upper crust of the river bed to try to find an upward water supply. If they succeed in doing this their eggs are then deposited in water which is perfectly pure and which is springing into the river course from the surrounding water table. With it comes a sufficient supply of oxygen. This may be difficult to understand, so here are the facts and the explanation as I see it.

A natural river course runs in the lowest part of the valley, but it is in fact only the visible part of a huge table of water which extends on either side. Water drains from the high lands to pass beneath the soil in the meadows, and under pressure it should enter the river course through a porous bed. If for any reason the bed of the stream has become solidified, as was the case with the upper Avon, any percolation from the water table is from the sides of the water course, from, in fact, beneath the banks where there is no access for spawning trout. I do not wish to create the impression that water gushes from the river bed in any great volume, but it does rise under pressure sufficient to counteract the pressure of the water travelling in the channel and to cause it to mingle with it, provided the natural course has not been obstructed by human agency.

This brings us to the matter of dams. Water can spring through a porous bed only if the pressure of water travelling over it is less than the pressure in the water table at either side. So the impounding of a stream prevents percolation by increasing pressure on the bed.

In our work on the upper Avon we have used bulldozers and dragline excavators on an extensive scale, and that we have found the answer to successful trout production is due more to luck than good planning. In trying to clear the fishery of vast accumulations of mud and silt, we scraped clean and broke up all our shallows, with the result that the water from the valley table is entering the course in many new places. In some reaches the level has been reduced considerably, so that now the river is running *in* the water table instead of *above* it.

The spawning trout are now placing their eggs where they have a supply of pure water, and this regardless of the condition of the water in the river channel. Instead of the redds becoming clogged with mud and silt forced into them by stream action, the upward currents from the bed are quite sufficient to keep all undesirable spoil, of which the upper Avon has a considerable amount, in suspension, and the eggs remain clean throughout the whole period of incubation instead of being slowly suffocated and dying after three or four weeks.

Chalk

When, after many years of study, experiments, hope and frustration, there is a possibility of success in a certain project it gives one a very nice feeling. As so often happens with anything really puzzling, when the light dawns and the answer is forthcoming it is so very simple. Immediately one wonders how it was possible to have been so blind – and others say at once, it is so obvious.

Something to combat and render innocuous the impurities which enter and have been entering our trout fisheries for many years has been in the thoughts of many. In recent years the evils caused by civilisation and general neglect have become more and more apparent. There are few streams left which are still in their pure and natural state and many I fear where the sport they provide must depend almost entirely on the introduction of ready-to-kill fish which have been bred and reared at great expense. The problem of trying to meet the demands of a large number of trout fishermen by the production of wild fish has been mine for nearly forty years. Though I have had some success, in the back of my mind was always the thought that it was a losing battle and that one day I would have to admit defeat.

To have healthy and good-sized wild sporting trout in a river, or for that matter in any water, means that these fish must have a pure, wholesome and abundant food supply. It is the provision of this that needs so much consideration, planning and perseverance.

Just because a river produces an abundance of the creatures one normally expects to become the food of trout is no reason to assume that these fish will eat them. The test of a good trout river comes, therefore, not from the number of animals to be found by dredging the bed or by searching the aquatic vegatation, but from the number and variety that are to be found in the stomachs of fish throughout the year. Autopsies on trout at regular intervals during a year can be very enlightening. Not only do they give one a good idea of the food taken during the different seasons, they also bring out the very important fact that trout can starve in water where the usual food animals exist in great quantities.

In the production of sporting-sized trout one has to consider them in two categories. There are those up to and perhaps just over two years old which can be satisfied with a diet of insect life and other small creatures. Then there are those of over two years old which, if they are to become fish of good sporting size and weight, must have food of a more satisfying nature. Many waters can provide a sufficiency of food in the form of insect life for these smaller fish but on such a diet they will grow to a certain size, to half a pound, perhaps three-quarters, but no larger. Such fish may be quite healthy and keep in fair condition but, even if they live for several years, neither length nor weight increases. To grow big fish, by this I mean fish of between one and two pounds, with some much larger, it is necessary to have big food for them which has a valuable protein content. In some waters, such as the chalk streams of the South Country, nature saw to it that such food could be available. I have in mind creatures such as snails, shrimps and crayfish. Individually, each is a body-builder and of great value. Where all three can be taken the value is increased. These, and indeed many other of the aquatic animals, can only be in abundance in water which has a high calcium content.

Though for many years I have suspected the quality of the food supply in the upper Avon of which I write, it is only during the past year* that I have been able to obtain anything factual to

*Written in 1964.

support my theories. My father and my grandfather lived beside the Avon and had interests in the fishing I look after. I had passed on to me all the knowledge I required as to what the Avon was like in the last century. My own observations go back for over fifty years and it is quite certain that in the old days the upper Avon water produced a much better average class of trout than it has done in the past generation. As I have said, I knew something was wrong and we have tried very hard to do something about it. The work carried out on the stretch of water belonging to the SDFFA under my supervision during the past ten years has had much publicity. No one can deny that great improvements have been made and that everything done has been well worth while. But the one aim I had has not so far been accomplished. We cleaned the river and adjacent streams. We produced trout and the food of trout in abundance, but still failed to get the big fish of years ago.

The increase in all aquatic life came, as was expected, soon after this big clean-up and it was this that was so puzzling. After a year or two the river teemed with the food required to produce really big trout but throughout the seasons autopsies proved that it was not taken by them. We had plenty of small trout, and they kept in very good condition while around ten or eleven inches in length. Some would grow larger than this but generally after the three-year-old stage, when most of our female fish spawn for the first time, they never seemed to regain their former plump condition. Weight for length of the majority was well below the average for the trout from a chalk stream. Though we got a fair number of quite good fish each year we were always hoping for a change. Each season was finished with a very good stock of fish just under eleven-inch takeable size. When I saw these fish in the spring there was little difference, and I would then think that richer feeding during the summer would make them grow, but it seemed a forlorn hope. And so it went on until the summer of 1963.

A Watercress Bed
With no real thought that it would be of any great value excepting as a reservoir to hold a pure and constant supply of water for my trout hatchery, in the late summer and early autumn of 1962 we dredged out an old watercress bed and

constructed in its place a small lake of about 1¼ acres. It is in elongated form, with the widest part about forty yards. In years past the cress beds had been fed with water from a series of deep springs which rise from the chalk in the bed, and to one side there rises a great chalk cliff which for generations had served as the main chalk-pit in our locality. We dredged to a depth of just over seven feet at one end before biting into chalk and gravel. This depth of spoil gradually shallowed until at the other end we were down to chalk at about three feet. The spring-water supply has always been constant and is entirely separate from the main river. The cress beds had been neglected for over fifty years and little was left to trace their origin. The site had become an oozy bog, with small pools of water around the spring holes.

As was to be expected in boggy ground there were quite a number of gnats and midges. Their larvae were numerous in the little pockets of water. In some of the deeper holes were shrimps, with occasional water boatmen and the water hog-louse. In one place where, in a previous experiment, we had constructed a small pond were a dozen or so trout of from a half to three-quarters of a pound.

The dredging was completed by the 10 October. I make mention of this date as I feel it is important. In our excavating efforts the chalk in the bed was churned up considerably and it was several weeks before this chalk fell from suspension and the water cleared sufficiently for the bottom to be seen.

During the 1962–3 winter, even when it was so bitterly cold, I was surprised to see the bed of the lake gradually becoming covered in algae, the bright green algae I always associate with highly alkaline and pure water and which produces the plankton which is so valuable in all trout waters. This continued to increase despite the fact that most of the lake was frozen over for nearly a fortnight. In the spring the whole bed was a bright green and I could see that the water was producing a multitude of gnats and midges. This vast production of both algae and chironomids continued throughout the summer and on occasions when they hatched the whole surface of the lake was covered by the empty larval shucks.

A Sunny Morning
In early August I noticed also that there had been a considerable

multiplication of shrimps as well as other creatures. From time to time I had seen odd trout rise but had given little thought to them until one bright sunny morning when there was no wind to ripple the surface and I could see the size of the fish making such dainty rings. It seemed impossible and, thinking the clear water acted to magnify the size, I went home for a rod and a box of nymphs. I wish to explain before going further that it was quite impossible for other fish to enter this small lake from the river as the outfall had been screened. Those in the lake in early August were the few which were present when we had finished dredging the previous October.

Using a pheasant tail artificial on a No. 13 hook I caught three of the trout and was broken by two others. I have seen many wild trout from a large number of rivers and lakes about the world but never any in the same condition as these three. Each looked more like a roach than a trout in shape and the bellies of all three were packed full of shrimps and gnat larvae. The weights in relation to length were as follows: first fish, 1 lb 10 oz, length 13½ inches; second, 1 lb 14 oz, length 14 inches; third, 3 lb, length 16 inches. The flesh of each had the colour of a fresh-run salmon with a taste equally good. In ten months one trout had grown from three-quarters of a pound to three pounds and in the lake were two others at that time which I knew were even larger.

Fine Condition

What is of greater importance is to explain just how these fish could grow to such weights and such fine condition in so short a time. This small lake was constructed in the Avon valley flat within ten paces of the main river and so it is true to say that the geological formation of the bed is identical. The springs which supply the water for it are but a few of those in this general locality which have always fed the river. So it is true to say the river has always had the benefit of these spring sources, though only after the water had seeped and meandered about the boggy ground where the rot of varied vegetation had been continuous. The reach of river adjacent to the lake varies considerably in depth but generally it corresponds very favourably with the lake, with parts up to six or seven feet in depth. Both river and lake are open to the sunlight. Yet in the adjoining reach of the main river, where the food supply for many years has been at least twenty times greater and considerably more varied than in the lake, not one trout of over a pound in weight was taken in 1963 and very few during the past five years.

For many years I have studied the trout and, indeed, the general aquatic life in this particular stretch. It is the home beat, so to speak, and therefore has claimed far more than its share of my attention when I have been in the mood for experiments. It is a water where crayfish are extremely numerous and where shrimps and molluscs are in multitude. Insect life too, of every known chalk-stream species, is in this water, together with an excellent stock of small trout. There are few grayling and fewer coarse fish. Here in this stretch and its feeder streams I had tried all I knew to get trout to grow big under natural conditions, but all without success until now.

I have tried impounding to create a lake effect and have given the river its free and natural flow – always without the desired effect. Trout would grow well and appear to be perfectly healthy until they attained a length of ten or eleven inches. Autopsies over the past ten years have proved that these trout fed almost exclusively on insect life. Never at any time of the year – though there was such an abundance – were any to be found with their bellies full of crayfish, shrimps or snails.

This reach was dredged, bulldozed and cleaned thoroughly in 1954–5. For two years after that there was a decided improvement in all classes of food. It was after this that the crayfish began to multiply to great numbers. They continue to thrive to the present time.* Our hopes for improvement in the general size of trout started to be realised but faded out. Why was it that these trout continued to starve where food was so plentiful? There could be only one answer and this I knew. The bed was still foul and the food produced on it was not palatable. Though plentiful, it was not of a sufficiently high standard of purity to be acceptable to fish as clean-living as trout. Why are conditions so different in the small lake? Again, there is but one answer. The water supply and the food produced on the bed of the lake are absolutely pure. One thing only has made this possible. And that is chalk.

---

*They have now (1984) been destroyed by the crayfish plague.

I am firmly convinced that the answer to our trout-fishery problems lies in chalk and after I have explained things as best I can, I feel sure you will think so too. Chalk has figured so prominently in all that has happened here during the past year that there can be no possibility of an error on my part. In lime we have nature's purifier and its benefit is well known in agriculture. It is time its value was better understood in pisciculture, too. Where a soil is acid or sour an application of chalk will sweeten it. The same kind of application can do the world of good to sweeten a trout water. Calcium is needed to create certain animal life, to break down the impurities, and for the well-being of much of the aquatic life we value in a trout fishery. Sometimes a considerable amount is needed.

Sour and Acid

For generations there has been much talk in the fishing world about the chalk streams. They were not named chalk streams by accident. It is generally assumed that being in chalk country the water of a river should be highly alkaline. How very far from the truth this is at the present time! In many chalk streams the ph value is down to a low level for the acidity and varied animal life produced by tons and tons of impounded and rotting vegetation has had too great a demand. Where an analysis of water is made I think people forget that all the animal life has to live on the bed. Though water travelling along might have a fair alkaline content, the bed can be quite sour and acid.

[*In 1962 and 1963 the river authorities were dredging the bed of the Avon above Sawyer's water, and a large pipeline was being laid in the valley. These activities resulted in large amounts of chalk being carried many miles down the river, in suspension*]

Clearance of the water took place very rapidly and I was amazed just how quickly the film over everything on the bed was absorbed, but more of this later. Proof that fly hatches were affected came on many occasions. It became very obvious that as soon as the water became thick with chalk all insects stopped hatching and only occasional fish would rise. Then, an hour or so after the river cleared again, flies would appear once more and fish begin to rise. None of the insects seemed to have been affected; they hatched quickly in the clear water and took flight without any signs of distress. Spinners came back to lay eggs but

164

here again it was very noticeable that egg laying took place only when the water was clear. Proof that the chalky water had no ill effect on the gills of trout had of course been established in the lake but I got plenty of further evidence when seeing trout emerge from the area of pump discharges and immediately start to rise to fly in the clear water upstream.

I had plenty of opportunity for repeated studies for though the River Board completed their programme in the spring we continued to get chalky water pumped into the river all through the summer and autumn, although not in such volume or so consistently. From early August onwards our hatches of small fly improved considerably and far more trout were to be seen. Our rods began to catch more fish and to report that these were of much better size and condition than in former years. It was then that the full significance of chalk became apparent to me. Having in mind the amazing growth of the trout in our small lake, I began to wonder if we were on the verge of a break-through with the river. Had the trout in the river started to show the same effects? Had the chalky water brought about the very thing I had wanted for so long? It was early days to be too hopeful but everything pointed that way. From August on through September and October I could see the trout were putting on weight. Some I caught were full of crayfish and shrimp. Ten- and eleven-inchers moved on rapidly to twelve and fourteen inches. Bellies deepened, while the river looked healthier than it had at any time in my memory.

Anxious to confirm what I had seen, it was decided to carry out our annual electric fishing for pike a little earlier than usual. This was at the end of September. I knew of several pike throughout the six miles of the fishery and as this was a period when we had been free from chalky water for a while I thought we would have a good chance of getting them. Though this was important I must confess that I was very keen to catch and examine some of our trout throughout the fishery. Electric fishing is a method which brings trout out from all manner of hiding-places and with this apparatus, if one has the power and is so inclined, it is possible to see almost every fish there is in a given stretch of river.

We got the pike and I saw all I wanted to of the trout. I had not been mistaken for in the fishery, as a result of the added calcium, were trout of sizes and condition I had been wanting all my life as a keeper. We killed about thirty for the different farmers with land beside the river. These fish had an average weight of 1½ pounds. Each had its belly packed full with crayfish and shrimps. Here was the evidence I had been seeking so long. Taking fish with the electrical apparatus gives one a chance to get a true idea of what the majority are feeding on. Those caught with a fly rod might for a short period be having a diet of insects. Consequently, all one would find in them would be insects in various stages. We saw a number of trout of between two and three pounds which I had not the heart to kill and examine. Each had its belly fully extended and a few I handled had the unmistakable crunchy feeling of crayfish inside. Incidentally, one of these large fish was taken on a nymph shortly afterwards. It weighed three pounds three ounces. Several big eels, each around three pounds, had crayfish in them, too.

I must confess to feeling very excited and indeed proud to be able to show off these trout. I knew the water of the Avon valley could produce worthwhile sporting trout if only I could find out what had been lacking in the past few years which was present long ago. Time and again I had been beaten and yet the answer is so very simple. A chalk stream must be a chalk stream if it is to live up to its high tradition. It was chalk and chalk alone which set such a high standard on the South Country streams of years ago. Though neither knew it, it was chalk which produced the big trout of which my father and my grandfather, and indeed others of their time, were so proud to talk. And it is chalk which can do it again. For my part I had been running around in circles blind to the fact that the very thing wanted is to hand in unlimited quantity.

The Hatchways

Of course, there was more calcium in the water and the river bed of years ago. So many things immediately come to mind in support. In the days of milling and irrigation hundreds of tons of chalk were carried into the meadows each year to make up the banks and the hollows, the hatchways and the river paths. Chalk was scattered here and there into the sour parts while the river bed and the beds of the feeder streams all had attention to keep them clean. No spoil of an undesirable nature was allowed to enter into the river and no chance given for any bulk to accumulate and cause acidity. In addition, pure chalk-water ran down from the hills after every shower. Year in and year out the river course received continuous replenishment of chalk and in those days there was little pollution which could sap and absorb its value.

Today the need for calcium in the trout waters is far greater than ever it was in my grandfather's day. Civilisation has added a tremendous burden with polluting matter and the purifier must be regulated accordingly. It is not a question of just neutralising the effects but of adding sufficient to become the master. Such mastery lies within our power. For many years there has been the story that lime will quickly kill fish and other aquatic life and this I fear has led many to the wrong conclusion. I must explain before going further that the lime from which such stories originated is quick, or unslaked, lime. It is true that this, tipped into water and brought into suspension, will quickly absorb all oxygen and bring about the death of aquatic creatures by suffocation. Natural chalk powder has just the reverse effect. Instead of absorbing oxygen it quickly creates it, so much indeed that it can help to break down the impurities arising from most of the decay of nature.

I know now that I should have discovered just how beneficial chalk can be a long time ago for there have been so many indications. When we bulldozed and draglined the whole fishery in our efforts to remove the vast accumulations of spoil and filth we did of course churn up much of the chalk in the river bed, more especially on the shallows. I thought afterwards that the great increase in all river life which followed on from these operations was due to the general clean-up. This no doubt was contributory but I now feel sure that the greatest value came from the disturbance of the chalk. Had we continued year after year to break up and disturb the chalk in the bed and send continuous flushes of suspended calcium throughout the fishery, I feel sure the general improvement would have been progressive. We must remember that many years ago the cleaning of shallows with horse and harrow was a recognised annual job in many rivers.

In the normal course of events the chemicals in solution, or in a river bed, should be ample to deal with all vegetation grown;

indeed, despite the enormous crops produced in the Avon each year, our water here could do its work but for the additional burdens it has to carry. But for these burdens there would not be the great need for the introduction of chalk. Long ago I came to the conclusion that the main trouble in the majority of our trout waters has been brought about by the lack of thought of our forefathers in planting trees beside the river. Leaves shed into a stream have done far more harm through the years than many of the minor industrial effluents or sewage wastes. Though few realise it, a heap of decomposing leaves is just as toxic as a heap of green grass. There has been considerable attention drawn to the poisonous effect of discharges of liquid from silage heaps; it is time more thought was given to a pollution which has been going on for generations. Some leaves are a much greater menace than others. Those which still carry their sap when they fall after the first frost are the chief offenders, for most of them sink immediately to the river bed. They are heavy and, if the stream is of the slow, meandering type, they get swept into heaps about the bed, there to remain until decomposed completely, when the fragmentation can lift into suspension and so be carried with the currents.

One can pile up a big heap of aquatic vegetation in a river and slowly though surely it is eaten away, finally to be dispersed by the running stream in a matter of a few weeks. A similar-sized pile of leaves may take a year, perhaps longer, before being broken down and even then there will be a residue of heavy, oily mud left which needs a very strong current to disperse it. Where this oily mud lies no aquatic life of value can exist. Often, such a heap is only partially decayed before another season's layer of leaves adds to it. The process has to start all over again. The decay is brought about by chemicals in solution and not by action from the river bed and so, though the outside of a heap can be broken down, the inside may still be in a state of fermentation.

During the past autumn and winter I have had every chance to see just what effect additional calcium can have to bring about complete breakdown of leaves in a small stream where the overhang of various kinds of trees caused the bed to be carpeted by a thick layer. Here in this stream great banks of mud had formed and on these various plants had grown to consolidate them. A half-mile upstream from this, a building site, which meant the excavation of many hundreds of tons of chalk, had been taking shape and this chalk had been dumped into boggy ground adjacent to the stream course. Some had been spilled into the water and, in an endeavour to clear the stream course, a bulldozer was used to push it out again. In consequence, much chalky water was carried downstream to where the leaves lay thickly on the bottom. The whole bed, leaves and growing plants, became covered in a thick, white film. In less than two months not a leaf could be seen and much of the spoil beneath the growing weedbeds had gone. The bed of the stream became clean and bright and, a month later, first-class algae started to grow.

This same kind of thing has been happening in our main river. Rotting vegetation of all kinds is being dealt with slowly and surely. I have had all the proof I require that chalk can bring our water back to its old-time state of purity.

In 1964, a series of four small artifical lakes were constructed beside the Avon, the intention being to provide an alternative kind of fishing to the river.

Excavation of this series of ponds started with the provision of a clean discharge ditch running close and parallel to the river. The outlet to this passes beneath an old mill site and falls into the old mill-stream at a much lower level than the lakes and the impounded river. As we progressed with the dredging of the first lake so a certain discharge of water came from the springs and the water table, and a slow, though steady, flow passed along the ditch to enter into the mill-tail.

We had completed but half of this first lake when to my surprise and pleasure I noticed that a migration of snails was taking place. They came from the main river and all along the ditch from the outfall to the top there was a steady procession of full-grown snails. These were of a species well known to me, *L. peregra*. Day after day the procession continued and all the while many thousands could be seen moving slowly but relentlessly upstream towards, and entering, the newly made lake.

From that moment I knew that we would be successful in our venture to produce good trout and I knew just what was attracting the snails. Here, indeed, was more evidence of the value of chalk. Long before it happened I knew what to expect.

These snails were all mature and were ready to spawn. Very soon masses of eggs were present on every conceivable thing in the water. Food production for trout had commenced.

I knew, too, that very soon food production for the snails would start also – and it did. Within a couple of weeks of the lake being dredged, algae started to form on the bottom and sides. It is of interest to note that snails were the first animals to be attracted to this new water. Others came, it is true, but much later on.

As we progressed with the construction of the four lakes so it became more and more obvious that snails would form a very substantial part of the food supply for trout. In a few weeks the eggs had hatched and tiny snails were in multitudes everywhere. It had been my intention to stock the lakes artificially with food animals collected from the river. Now I knew there was no need. Nature was doing it for me and on a scale with which I could not hope to compete. The fourth lake was not completed until April 1965, and shortly after this we introduced a mixed bag of six-inch trout. Five hundred of these were rainbows and the other five hundred were browns.

These were put into the three lakes which had been completed in 1964. My previous experiments of stocking with rainbows in the upper Avon had not been very successful and stocking with these now was more of an experiment than with any real hope of them becoming big fish. Because I was very doubtful, despite the migration of snails, if sufficient time had elapsed to build up a food supply large enough for a thousand fish, it was decided to supplement this by feeding once a day with pellets. A start was made with four pounds a day, later on increasing to six pounds a day. This feeding went on until the end of September 1965.

Both brownies and rainbows grew fast. At the end of September, roughly six months after they were introduced as six-inch stock, I caught and killed two of the rainbows. Each of these weighed 1½ pounds and measured 13½ inches. In the lakes were others which I estimated to be quite two pounds. Such growth amazed me but after making autopsies on the two I killed there was enlightenment. The whole of their insides from throat to vent were packed full of snails.

How the Chalk was Applied to the Main River
Applications with both powdered and lump chalk were carried

out twice here in 1964, and twice in 1965. For the lump chalk we hired a mechanical apparatus which has a digging scoop at the back and a big shovel at the front. This was used to dig and to pulverise the chalk as finely as possible in pits which are adjacent to the river at two separate points. When the chalk was dug and crushed, the machine was able to scoop it up in the front shovel and then carry it in loads of about half a ton to dump into the river. The places we chose for the dumping were in fast-running parts where stream forces could work continuously in scouring the loose fragments. In this way the chalk powder contained in the loads came gradually into suspension, to be carried with the currents and to be deposited further downstream. Our fishery extends to just over six miles and, of the two points chosen for the dumps, one was near to the upper boundary and the other about mid-way down.

The dumping of the freshly dug chalk was carried out in April of each year and left untouched until early August. Then, with a gang of men using various tools, the chalk was loosened and spread more thinly so that the finer fragments and dissolved matter could be carried down river. The disturbance thus caused ensured a flow of chalky water which was carried in suspension for quite two miles downstream. On each occasion in 1964 and 1965 an estimated total of fifty tons was introduced to each place.

In addition to the local chalk we obtained four separate ten-ton loads of powdered chalk, supplied dry in plastic bags, from a firm which deals in this kind of thing for agricultural purposes. These loads were distributed in even parts all along the fishery at approximately half-mile intervals. Two loads were introduced in April and early August 1964 and a similar quantity at the same times in 1965. In all, this made a total of forty tons.

With the first delivery in April 1964, we did our best to give the whole river a light dressing with the powdered chalk. For this, a boat was used in which up to six hundredweight could be drifted downstream and scattered thinly by a man working with a shovel. Though an even dressing was accomplished this took much longer than I had anticipated and meant the employment of three men. After loading, it needed a man at either side of the river to hold the boat with ropes, while the third shovelled out the chalk. It was a costly, laborious, and rather messy business.

I decided, therefore, to try out a second method and this was to have the powder tipped straight into the river in the fast-running parts and leave it to be dispersed gradually by the water. I have found this to answer very well in the running stream and it saved much work and expense.

The chalk powder is very slowly dissolved into the water supply and I found that, at every half-mile, there was a good link-up with the powder which came immediately into suspension. Generally, the whole river gets just as good a dressing as when it is scattered from a boat. The only advantage gained in using a boat is that liberal dressings can be given to places where mud is present.

On several reaches we have impounds where a set of sluice gates controls the flow of the river. Here I found it to be a good plan to pour the chalk powder slowly into the water being forced through a hatchway. This ensured a very quick mix as the chalk hit the pressurised flow, and the suspended matter was soon swept away to the reach below, where it spread evenly from bank to bank.

So much for distribution. Generally, one might say it is quite a simple operation. The main expense lies in procuring the chalk and getting it to the river. Once in the water, much of it is disturbed and scattered in a natural way. Discoloration of the water is of very short duration. A dense flush takes place immediately after introduction but within an hour or so all is quite clear, even just below the dumps.

For a day or two after applications are made the river bed, and all vegetation growing on it, is covered with a white film. Then this disappears and the bed and plants regain their former appearance. Interference with fishing is of very brief duration. With applications such as these there is no danger of putting down trout or grayling for any length of time.

On one occasion in 1964 I met one of our fishermen a couple of hours after we had introduced a dozen bags of chalk powder to a certain shallow. He was delighted for, when the river cleared he killed two brace of good trout on dry fly and these only a hundred yards or so downstream.

The freshly dumped chalk soon becomes populated with aquatic animals. Numbers of these no doubt are in the area of river bed on which the chalk is scattered and just bore their way up through it to the surface. Larvae and nymphs of insects are quickly in evidence, to be followed soon afterwards by hordes of shrimps and caddis. Then one sees scores of loach and bullheads with, here and there, a crayfish. A shoal of minnows may explore the new territory and then trout and grayling appear. All show up very plainly on the white background.

A few days will pass and then some of the chalk changes colour to green as algae starts to form on it. Later on, hordes of small snails will cluster on all the lumps, many showing like black specks on the white surface. I have counted as many as 150 tiny snails on a knob of chalk no larger than my fist. As the days pass so numbers increase until the whole mass of chalk is tenanted by a great variety of creatures.

The action of the introduced chalk in the dispersal of mud is evident in less than a month. As the weeks pass along so the evidence increases. Mud disappears. I know I have been called severely to task and, indeed, ridiculed for stating that the 'chalk gradually ate its way into big deposits of evil mud, slowly though surely reducing them'. I realise this was descriptive rather than fact. But it does happen in that way.

I still maintain that the mud is eaten away gradually but have come to the conclusion that it is not any direct chemical action of the chalk which does this, as I thought was happening then, but instead that it is the result of a multitude of animal life that is created, fostered or encouraged by the carbonate of lime.

Here again I would welcome aid in solving this problem, for I can go so far and no further without scientific or biological help. What I think is happening is that certain creatures feed on the organic matter; that, after the mud has passed through the bodies of these animals, so the weight of it is reduced considerably and the matter can then rise easily into suspension to be carried away by the most gentle of currents. This, I would think, is what nature intended should happen, and it is from the naturalist's point of view that I put forward this theory.

However, I intend to leave this for others to sort out. If I am ridiculed again, I do not mind. There must be some answer to account for the fact that since we began our chalk activities many hundreds of tons of mud have disappeared. Still more is going as time passes. There are places where formerly mud was present up to three feet in depth. Now there is clean gravel.

Effect on Water Plants

My observations in past years have proved that of the fifty or so common plants there are but seven which are of real value in trout production. I record them according to my views as to their merit: 1 water celery (*Apium nodiflorum*); 2 water parsnip (*Sium erectum*); 3 watercress (*Nasturtium officinale*); 4 starwort (*Callitriche stagnalis*); 5 river dropwort (*Oenanthe fluviatilis*); 6 mares-tail (*Hippuris vulgaris*); and finally, the water buttercups (*Ranunculus spp*).

From a food point of view there is little to choose between water celery and water parsnip. Both are loved by shrimps and crayfish, and, in a rather lesser degree, by snails, throughout the year. Watercress has its greatest attraction when it starts to decay after the first frosts in the autumn, and this is true to a certain extent with the water parsnip. Both, then, have great value.

With water celery there is a difference. This is a plant where decay and growth will continue throughout the year and it was for this reason I gave it primary place in my table. It is a plant which needs considerable calcium if it is to keep healthy and produce its customary fine green beds in the winter as well as in other seasons of the year. It is now finding conditions satisfactory in the upper Avon.

In the late autumns of 1963, 1964 and 1965, after the first frosts, I pulled out a lot of the decaying masses of watercress and water parsnip to give the currents a chance to sweep along beneath the banks and carry away any decomposed matter. While doing this I had to be continuously picking up crayfish and putting them back into the river. Snails and shrimps manage to regain the water themselves if the bulk is not pulled too far from the river edge. Crayfish often become stranded and die if not assisted.

In 1963, while pulling out this rubbish, I collected over a thousand crayfish to stock one of our lakes where I had been building up a food supply.

Mayflies and other Insects

It is nice to have a mayfly season on any river, but nothing to my mind is more discouraging than to see thousands of flies on and about the water and yet not a single fish interested in them.

174

Some say it is because the fish get surfeited. This might be true sometimes, but on various occasions I have taken trout when they have been acting in this way. These have risen for a time or two and then gone down. After a while they start again to take two or three flies and then no more.

As I have said, I have caught such fish. Far from being surfeited, there have been no mayflies in their stomachs at all. If this is not proof that they have no liking for the flies after they have taken them, I fail to see what other conclusion one can reach. I repeat what I have said many times before – trout will only take insects in the nymph and dun stage if these have been living in a wholesome environment.

Eagerness on the part of trout to take floating flies and nymphs was very evident in September. It is a very welcome time when you can see fish taking everything within their sight which they think is a fly or a nymph.

Other Creatures
To me river life is not all beneath the surface and creatures other than the aquatic ones can be indicators of whether a trout water is in good shape or not. It is a fact, indeed, that there are a number whose lives depend on the purity of water and one of these is the dabchick or little grebe.

There are many, I know, who consider this little diving bird to be a pest in a trout stream and I agree that where there are great numbers of them they can be a nuisance. But I feel, too, that all who own trout waters should be thankful that their fishery is considered by this little bird to be worth living on, and in. The dabchick lives almost exclusively on subaqueous food and, though its diet is somewhat varied, all this must be of a first-class nature.

Any trout water where dabchicks were once numerous and have disappeared can well be examined thoroughly for trouble. These water birds will not stay long on any water unless conditions are favourable for themselves and for their young. I can say with very good reason that wherever dabchicks are plentiful good fish will be found.

Years ago dabchicks were very plentiful along the upper Avon but since the last war their numbers had gradually decreased. We had got to the stage when there were, perhaps, a couple of pairs to the mile and that was all. No one to my knowledge interfered with their nests but no full clutches of young were produced. This went on until the year we started with our chalk applications and in the two years since there has been a tremendous multiplication. It is possible that in the near future some control of the numbers will have to be made.

I feel sure the increase could not possibly have come about by the successful breeding of the few pairs we had as residents in so short a time. I think it likely that many have migrated to our water from other reaches. Dabchicks can fly long distances when they feel so inclined.

Dabchicks are good indicators but a second creature which owes its livelihood to wholesome conditions in a river is the water-vole. To my way of thinking these interesting and attractive little mammals are a part of the riverside. It is true they do some harm in burrowing and undermining banks but rather than be vexed about this one should feel pleased they are there to enjoy their natural food. Water-voles are mostly vegetarian. A very high proportion of their food is taken beneath the surface and consists of aquatic plants.

The production and health of these plants is as important to the vole as is the aquatic animal life to the dabchick. During the past two years water-voles have increased considerably. To me the sight of them is a welcome one for I can well remember the years around 1950 when our main river was deserted by them, which added to the sorrow I had at that time in trying to look after a fishery that was dying through the carelessness or thoughtlessness of others.

Be thankful, therefore, the voles are on hand to be a part of the riverside. Bless them as they sit munching strands of weeds by their holes in the banks and welcome them as they come swimming across the stream. I feel we should think more kindly of others, too. The past two years have brought about a great increase in the population of moorhens.

To me a river without a moorhen is like a farmyard without a fowl. Like the water-vole, the moorhen is mostly vegetarian, but whereas both the vole and the dabchick get their food from on, or near, the bottom, most of that taken by the moorhen is from, or near, the surface. This does not mean they are less selective. The food of the moorhen must be of a high standard and though these waterfowl may be seen in various places where there is water they are not likely to remain if the food they wish to take is tainted in any way by pollution.

Moorhens have been present in the Avon valley for as long as I can remember but it is only in the past two years that they have become numerous and likely to become too prolific for the peace of some of our fishermen. I must say I don't feel very kindly towards a moorhen which scuttles out from the bank and puts down a good trout I have been stalking, but rather this than no trout and no moorhen, for if one is sufficiently patient the fish will start to rise again as it must know there is no reason to be scared for long.

Never throughout my life on the river have I seen kingfishers in such number as are now present along the upper Avon. At one time I thought kingfishers were like robins in having a territory of their own and this I judged to be a stretch of about half a mile. But this is not true now.

There must be at least a dozen birds to every mile of the valley and, far from being rare, as many people think, I see numbers each day. I hope the time will never come when some control is necessary with kingfishers, for, apart from hawks, I know of no creature which will make a prey of them.

Here is another example of one thing leading to another. In the first place algae is created, then come various planktonic animals. Following these is an abundance of sticklebacks, and then kingfishers. Kingfishers are very fond of young stickle-backs, before they are fully grown and have produced an array of stiff spines on the dorsal fin.

At all stages in growth until they are fully mature, sticklebacks will live at peace together in great shoals. Throughout the year, and seemingly regardless of weather and water conditions, these shoals can be seen at the edges of a stream, or poised near the surface in parts which are less rapid and deeper. They can be very easy prey for kingfishers and I would say have really good food value for them.

But from beauty let us move on to something more sombre, for this is how I think of coots. We have never had many coots in the upper Avon valley and I cannot say I am sorry. Coots are a much hardier species than either moorhens or dabchicks but even they will forsake a badly polluted area. I think they have insides which are less queasy and can feed in water which moorhens and dabchicks have forsaken. In many respects the feeding habits of the coot are like those of the dabchick, for a very high proportion of its food is subaqueous.

Usually you will find coots in stretches where coarse fish abound and I feel there is a point about this which might be considered. When a water becomes unfit for trout to live in or thrive in, then coarse fish take over. These can take food of a much inferior character. It is the same with coots, moorhens and dabchicks. The first take up residence after the other two consider conditions to be unsuitable.

To a certain extent coots are like mallard and will feed anywhere it is wet. However, mallard are no indicators of anything good or bad. I have known duck to live and feed quite happily in conditions where an introduced trout could not possibly live more than a few moments. But duck coming in frequently to the shallow parts of a trout stream indicate a certain food supply.

They are very fond of freshwater snails and where any water is producing an abundance of these molluscs duck will become a nuisance. Fortunately, we are not worried overmuch with duck. The upper Avon valley is far too public for these wildfowl to take up residence and though some fly in at dusk from other parts of the river a few deaths caused by someone waiting with a gun soon makes sure that no heavy inroad is made into the snail population. They are easy to discourage, in fact, and I wish the same could be said of swans.

Swans, even in small numbers, are a menace in any fishery, whether this is a game or a coarse-fishing one. I wish I could say that our chalk applications have discouraged these interlopers, for that is how I consider them. Unfortunately, it is just the reverse. It would almost seem that word has been passed along to all swans in the Avon valley that there is a free-for-all of good-class feeding in our stretch. It was bad enough in the winter of 1964–5 but the past one of 1965–6 was even worse.

They came in such numbers that nothing less than an army of machine-gunners could have made much impression or driven them away, and I despaired of trying. It is fortunate in a way that a pair of swans insist on having a territory of their own during the breeding season and usually this represents quite half a mile of the valley.

Having staked his claim, so to speak, in the spring, the old cob rides roughshod over any who try to dispute it, or want to live on the same reach of water. So for a time at least we have but a pair to every half-mile.

Herons seem to be quite unaffected by any of our work. Always there has been some fluctuation in their numbers but at no time have they been a nuisance or a menace. Though herons like to take and eat trout and indeed can do damage during a spawning season, they seem to be just as happy on waters where no trout exist at all. Now, though I have come to hate the sight of swans, I still have admiration for the heron, Old Stalky as I call him.

In a way I would feel quite happy if I had done something to help him and his family. At least he will clear off when he sees me about, even though his right at the riverside is far greater than mine, or indeed of any human. If swans were less truculent and also cleared off on seeing me I could be more tolerant towards them. It is their attitude in taking things for granted which riles me so much.

In the spring and throughout the summer of 1965 we had more swifts, swallows and martins in the valley than for many years. I know these birds, and others too, take a big toll of our aquatic flies, but I think it is heartening to see them busy over the water. It is a first-class sign of river purity when hordes of these migrants, and other insect-catching species, elect to come and stay in a stretch of valley and produce their young.

Old birds can live on second-, or even third-class food, but young ones must have the best if they are to thrive. And so to me it was a very welcome sight to see the heads of four or five young swallows or house martins peeping out from nests beneath the eaves of houses, and to hear young swifts in their holes in the thatch, and young sand martins around the chalk and the gravel pits. It was pleasing, too, when hordes of sparrows and chaffinches joined the flycatchers and wagtails, and indeed many other birds, to take advantage of the mayfly hatches.

It is so true to say that when the birds are eager to take the hatching flies, the fish are eager to take them also. It is a sorry sight, and I regret to say one I have witnessed on various occasions, when hordes of insects hatch and yet neither birds nor fish have the slightest desire to feed on them.

179

One can get quite a warm feeling in the heart when nature is prompted to take advantage of something you yourself have helped to create. When a river is in a healthy state there is plenty for all. I am not one of those who think fishing is all for the human. We should be prepared to share with those who have the greater right. It is true one gets a vexed sort of feeling when coming across the remains of a good trout left by an otter on the bank, or in seeing big fish with the unmistakable stab wound of a heron in shoulder or flank. But the way I look at it is this:

Better by far to see fish killed like this and know such trout were in the water and that others are still there in good numbers. Better by far to have otters and herons and know that they only visit the water for the goodness they can get, for a river, without all the natural bankside creatures, is indeed a sorry sight.

An ounce of anything which may help to bring about more healthy conditions and better aquatic life is worth many tons of pity that there are cases where such help is desirable.

NOTE

The series of articles on chalk caused a considerable stir. It was at once pointed out that there was no scientific proof for Sawyer's claims. He was the first to admit that he was no scientist; he was an experienced and acute observer, and a naturalist, and he reported what he had seen. Others complained that the chalk did not remove silt. Sawyer had never said that it did. He had only said that it would act to get rid of putrefying matter, such as decaying leaves.

His ideas created even greater interest in France, which also has chalk streams. All the articles were translated into French (by M. Raymond Rocher) and printed in *Plaisirs de la Pêche*. M. André Gagniard became interested and published an article in that magazine in 1975. He had worked on various ways of applying the powdered chalk. He advised putting plastic sacks in fairly slow-running water, and cutting slits in the sacks to allow the chalk to escape slowly. A special brand of high-quality chalk from the Champagne district of France was marketed under the name 'Nautex', and was widely used over there. It seems to have been yet one more case of a British idea being appreciated more overseas than at home.

As regards Sawyer's own upper Avon, the story is a sad one.

There has been no large-scale use of chalk since the sixties, nor a repeat of the fifties clean-up. It is too expensive now. Large numbers of trout are caught, but they are almost all hatchery-bred. Natural spawning is almost non-existent. There has been abstraction of water higher up, and greater use of chemicals on the land. The bed may be again compacted.

The valley is still beautiful and wildlife is still plentiful, but the fact that fish do not spawn is a sign that all is far from well.

sv

$$— 21 —$$

The Buried Treasure

I WILL TELL THE STORY just as I heard it from the owner of the bitch, and you must judge for yourselves. But first I must make a little explanation. At the farmhouse nearby is a rather eccentric old man of over seventy. He is the brother of the farmer's wife, and has been living with them for years. For ten years he has had a wire-haired terrier bitch, and the two are inseparable.

Somehow I think the bitch understood the old man better than any human companion, and he in turn thought the world of her. Now from time to time, as it is only natural that it should, this bitch would wander off for a few hours, perhaps all day, without, in the words of the old man, telling him where she was going. In her absence he was almost frantic, and would search the neighbourhood until he located her. This had happened several times and when, one day recently – it was a Monday – he told me she was again missing, I thought little about it, and assured him she would soon be home again.

I saw him on Tuesday and asked about the bitch. No, she had not returned; and, though he had searched everywhere and made inquiries, all that he could learn was that early on Monday morning she had been seen with the farm dog, an old black mongrel. Then they were heading towards a big rabbit burrow about a quarter of a mile from the farm. The farm dog had returned in the evening without the bitch.

When I saw the old man on the morning of Wednesday he looked ill and haggard. The bitch could not be found. He had hunted all day on Tuesday, until darkness made further search impossible. 'I prayed for her last night,' he said. 'I asked God to let me find her wherever she may be, and whether she be dead or alive.' He spoke with great depth of feeling and sincerity, and I could picture the scene as the old fellow knelt at his bedside asking that his friend might be found. It was pathetic, and I felt that this old man loved his bitch more than his own life.

I told him, more for consolation than anything else, that I would keep my eyes open in case she was anywhere along the river valley, and would bring her home if I did see her. Rather than witness more of the old man's misery, I left him and went on my way. Though I kept my promise to look around, I did not see the bitch.

Then came Thursday morning. I saw the old man some distance away from me, and he appeared years younger as he hastened towards me. 'I've found her,' he shouted, as he got nearer, his face beaming with joy. 'I've found her,' he repeated. 'And t'was God's own handwork. But I'll tell 'ee.' And he launched into this remarkable story.

'You know I told 'ee she went off with the farm dog up across to the big rabbit bury. Well yesterday I hunted high and low all day and then, after tea, I told my sister I would have one more look, and take old Nip, the farm dog, with me, as he might know where she were to.' I thought this a sensible thing to do and wondered why he had not done it in the first place. I thought I knew what was coming. But no. He told his story in his own way, omitting nothing.

'When I got to the gate leading to the rabbit bury, there was a car stopped there. I looked inside and there was a gun propped up in a corner. Somebody poaching I thought, and on the rabbit bury I could see the figure of a man. Straight away I went across to him and asked him what he was doing there. Looking for rabbits, he replied. So I told him he had no business to be there – that in fact he was poaching.

'Then it turned out to be somebody I knew several years ago, who then had permission from the farmer to shoot a rabbit sometimes. He had been away for a long time and had just returned to this locality, so was looking around to see if there were any rabbits about, before again asking for permission to shoot one. That's why his gun were in the car. Well I told him that I was looking for my little terrier, and had brought the old farm dog to help me. Had he heard anything in the bury, or seen my bitch? He hadn't.

'We searched along the bury and looked in the holes, while old Nip prowled about sniffin' yer and there. Then all of a sudden he said, "I've been up on the downs having a look round up there, but I didn't see anything of a dog. But I heard a fox killing a rabbit in one of the burrows up there." "What did 'ee say?" I asked. "Heard what?" And when he said it again I knew. "That wer no fox," I told him. "That's my bitch, I'll bet a pound. Where was it?"

'Well he told me as best he could but I couldn't make out where 'twas. "Here," I said, "will you do me a favour? Charge what you like, but take me up to that place in your car." "I'll take you up with pleasure," he said, "and I hope it is your dog. I don't want to be paid for doing it. Come on."

'So with the old farm dog I bundled into the car, and away we went. All the way along I had a feeling that what he'd heard was my terrier. If 'twas a fox or a badger in the hole, he were actin' main funny, for neither of 'em bark or whine when they be killin' a rabbit. If 'twas either badger or fox then it was in a trap, or jammed in so it couldn't get out. And the more I thought about it, the more sure I was that 'twas old Nell.

'Well, we went up the track, and over the downs for about two miles. I began to wonder if the bitch could have come all this way, when he pulled up by a bury. I scrambled out. "It was in that hole," he said. So I gets down and listens, but not a sound could I hear. "Nell," I shouted into the hole, "Nellie." And then I heard her. She was in there.

'The inside of the hole was all blocked up with chalk, so I pawed it out and tore up the ground to open out the hole, but I couldn't reach her, or see her. The hole went straight on down several feet, and gradually got deeper. "For the love of heaven what are we going to do?" I said to the man with me. "We must get her out. We must get a spade. Where can I get a spade?" So I says to him, "Will you do me another favour and go across to the aerodrome and borrow a spade, while I stop here and talk to her?"

"I'll see it through now I've started," he said, "if it takes us all night to find out what's in the hole." He didn't believe 'twere old Nell in there, but he went off in the car. It was getting dark, and I lay down by the hole talking to Nell, telling her I'd forgive her if she'd come out, and that I'd make her all better if she was ill. But she didn't come out.'

At this stage I could picture this pathetic old man, crouching at the hole entrance with the tears streaming down his weather-beaten face, entreating his friend to come out, hoping beyond hope that he had not been deceived, and now and then as he heard a whimper making frenzied attempts with his hands to tear off the turf, or to paw out some more chalk from the blocked entrance. An old man alone in the middle of thousands of acres of downland, with darkness fast approaching.

He went on: 'He seemed to be gone a long time, and I was afraid it would soon be too dark to do anything. I tore off some more of the turf. Then at last he came with a spade. I flung off my coat and dug and dug. It was hard chalk, but soon I was down to my waist in a big hole. He wanted to help, but I was afraid he'd hurt old Nell with the spade. And then I got down to the hole. I'd dug straight down to her and there was one of her hind legs moving under the chalk.

'I dived down head first and soon uncovered her other hind leg and then pulled her out through the loose chalk. I can't tell 'ee how pleased I was to see her. She was in a bad way, but she knew me. She knew I wouldn't leave her there to die. God had answered my prayers, for if this wasn't the handwork of God's own self, then what was it? He led I to her, and 'tis He I must thank. Yes, she's all right this morning, and, though that digging tired me out, I be well again.'

Well, there is the story and never have I heard anything to compare with it. The terrier had gone into the hole, probably following a rabbit. She had then pawed away the loose chalk to get still further into the hole, and the spoil she had removed had piled up behind her so that backward movement was impossible. Progress forward was barred by a firmer layer of chalk, and there she was trapped unable to move either way. It is possible that she had been there during the three days she had been missing, and there, but for human help, she would most certainly have died.

Now there is nothing unusual about a dog trapping itself in a hole like this, or in wandering off two or three miles hunting, but it is the circumstances that led to the finding of the bitch that I found so remarkable. In the first place, the old man acted entirely on impulse in deciding to have one last look round. Secondly, the man he met on the rabbit burrow had been away for years; he had no right on the downs, and, at this lonely spot, miles from the nearest human habitation, and amongst the thousands of rabbit burrows in these vast acres, his footsteps had been guided to the one hole that contained the bitch. Thirdly, the bitch had heard footsteps; she knew she was trapped, and had sense enough to try to attract attention by barking and whining. Then, most important of all, the old man had prayed that his friend might be found.

22

The Humane Trap

To: The Editor   1 February 1948
Sunday Express

I have been looking at the most pitiable sight in the world: the picture of a rabbit lying dead with its paw in a steel trap. Dead after a long night of torture.

The tragedy is in the creature's face: no longer the innocent, friendly face of a rabbit, but a face old and drawn and wise through suffering.

Surely, surely, sir, this terrible business must be stopped, this thing so horrible even in a picture. And the remedy is to hand in the Sawyer trap which kills instantaneously.

H. de Vere Stacpoole
Bonchurch, Isle of Wight.

SAWYER'S WORK on a humane trap to replace the gin spans the years from 1935 to 1958. It had its moments of triumph, and he succeeded in changing the law, but the anguish outweighed the joy and it ended in the bitterest of ironies.

Jim Perrett was an old gamekeeper who worked part-time on the river with Sawyer. He did a lot of rabbit trapping – as many country people did, for the rabbit was an important part of their diet – but he had no liking for the steel-toothed gin trap. 'It's a cruel way of catching the poor beggars,' he would say, 'but we got nothing else.' One day in 1935 he showed Sawyer a new trap. 'It won't catch rabbits,' he said, 'so why don't you try? The RSPCA are offering £300 to anyone who can invent a humane substitute for the gin.'

Sawyer's imagination was caught. He too hated the gin. He wrote: 'It sickened me to see rabbits struggling with their broken and bloodied legs gripped in the teeth of those steel jaws.' If his main motive was compassion, the work itself also appealed to him. He enjoyed working with his hands at a bench, especially when he could let his ideas have full rein. And the money was certainly a factor: £300 was a vast sum in those days to a man earning a little over £2 a week.

From 1935, every spare moment was spent in his garden shed working on the trap. He had a bench, a small vice, and hand tools – a hack-saw, files, hammer, and a hand drill. He had no forge or anvil, no way at all to heat metal. He went to dumps for metal, using parts of old perambulators. The springs which were so important to the design came from old bedsteads.

From the start, Sawyer's thoughts were directed towards a trap with arms like calipers, connected to a powerful spring. When the rabbit stepped on a small platform, the spring would be released by a trigger mechanism, closing on the animal's neck: the rabbit would be killed instantly. This was the theory, but, as anyone who has tried a little practical engineering knows, there is a large gap between theory and the finished product. There were over twenty moving parts in the trap, and a weakness in one caused the failure of the whole.

Sawyer contacted the RSPCA in 1936. They were interested and asked for a specimen trap for trial. It was spring, but they said that 'owing to the breeding season' they could not under-take trials until the autumn. Sawyer was wryly amused, knowing that rabbits breed all the year round. The first trials were promising, but the RSPCA expert, Mr Rodgers, found that the springs varied in strength. During that winter of 1936–7 Sawyer worked on improving the springs.

In 1937 the RSPCA wrote asking for twenty of the improved traps to test. Neither they nor any of the friends he approached were willing to share the financial burden, so at his own expense he found a firm in the Midlands who liked the prototype and would make the twenty for testing. They arrived, and in high excitement he took them out and set them in rabbit burrows. At dawn the next day he visited the traps to find they had been vandalised in the night. Of the twenty, eight had disappeared. Of the twelve left, four had dead rabbits in them. The others had been sprung and had traces of rabbit on them. He was bitterly upset at the setback, for apart from the theft of eight traps he knew that the design was wrong. The arms were set vertically and when closing they missed the animal's head; they ought to be set at a forward angle. This of course, meant redesigning the trap.

He wrote to the firm in the Midlands who were not pleased, saying that they had already set up jigs and tools. In the meantime, they enclosed their account for £37 – and if you are earning £2 a week such a letter is liable to upset your day, to say nothing of your wife's.

Margaret decided that she could not bear to see him suffering such frustration and disappointment. 'He took things to heart so.' So she persuaded him to give it up, and he reluctantly agreed. A few days later he came back from a walk in the meadows. He was carrying a gin trap, and in it was the severed leg of a fox. He explained that he had found the trap entangled in a barbed wire fence. The fox, trapped by the leg, had pulled in his frenzy until he had torn his leg completely off.

He held the sickening object up for Margaret to see and said, 'What are we going to do about this?' Margaret knew there was no other way but to tell him, 'Of course, you must go on with the work.'

Sawyer made some of the new traps and tested them with good results. In the summer of 1938, Mr Rodgers of the RSPCA came to Netheravon and gave the trap a thorough testing over a week. He went away impressed. During the rest of 1938, and the

189

summer of 1939, as Sawyer later learnt, the RSPCA were busy testing other traps, but in early September 1939 Rodgers came again to Netheravon with a number of traps to test against the Sawyer trap – which outclassed all the others. The RSPCA wrote to say that the results were highly promising but that 'owing to the outbreak of war all work in this direction must be postponed.'

Sawyer accepted the disappointment stoically, and got on with the war himself. In his job as a war reserve policeman at Netheravon he had long hours on duty when he could think of ideas for the trap and he continued to improve it. One of the snags had been the lack of a safety catch. Rodgers had complained of catching his fingers painfully in the trap. Sawyer solved this problem.

The war in Europe ended in May 1945, and in Asia in August 1945. Towards the end of that year, the RSPCA made contact with Sawyer again. He sent them some new traps, and the work was taken up where it had been left six years before. In 1946, he thought publicity would help and he wrote an article for *The Field*. There were a number of letters of interest and good wishes, but no offers of financial help, which he so sorely needed. On the contrary, a friend told him that he must patent his trap. This he eventually did, and it cost him the huge sum of £150.

In September 1946, the RSPCA held large-scale tests at Netheravon and while they were in progress representatives of the Pest Control Division of the Ministry of Agriculture, Fisheries, and Food, (MAFF) suddenly appeared on the scene and showed great interest. These tests were the most successful yet, and one of the RSPCA men whispered to Sawyer that he might be awarded the prize. He wrote:

'Now there was one from whom I could not possibly keep the news, and that was my wife. She had a lot to put up with through the years. It had been an uphill battle all the way, as much for her as for me – possibly much more, for she had our family to look after, and I had been spending money that I had no right to spend in the circumstances. I had neglected her in many ways. Maybe she will never realise what I had in my mind, for somehow I wonder now if I ever did myself. It was a blind desire to succeed, and I felt too, that if ever I did succeed I would be able to make up for all the hardships she and the youngsters had endured. A foolish thought, as I well know now.'

In the spring of 1947, the MAFF took a hand and Sawyer took part in comprehensive tests in Herefordshire. Despite appalling weather conditions, and Sawyer suffering from painful back trouble, the MAFF seemed impressed. Was the tide turning at last? At the end of May a letter arrived from the RSPCA saying that he had been awarded the £300 prize, which had been on offer since 1917 and which trained engineers with every facility had failed to win. He wrote: 'My wife looked across the table toward me with her eyes full of tears.'

He received his award from the Chairman of the RSPCA, Sir Robert Gower, in the Kingsway Hall, London on 26 June 1947. There was much publicity and he was showered with congratulations. The long trials and tribulations of the years since 1935 seemed to have ended in triumph. But it was illusory, for his real troubles were just beginning.

Later that year, the RSPCA offered to help with manufacture of the trap. They were naturally anxious to end the use of the gin, and they seemed to have got wind of the MAFF's interest. If they could keep the momentum going, the MAFF might take it on. There was a meeting at the RSPCA headquarters in Jermyn Street with Sawyer present, when it was decided in principle that the new trap must be competitive in price with the gin. It is easy to understand why they wanted this, but it was disastrous. All the future trouble stemmed from attempts to produce the trap on the cheap.

A firm in Birmingham was found to quote a reasonable price, and they agreed to make fifty traps for testing at Netheravon in September of that year, 1947. Sawyer took one look at them when they arrived and knew they were hopeless. The metal was plainly too flimsy and cheap: the action of the powerful spring would distort them. With heavy heart, Sawyer set the traps. The weather was ideal – dry and warm – and the first night nine traps out of twelve killed rabbits cleanly. During the second night there was heavy rain and the result was failure. The traps had distorted. Sawyer said that the trial was a farce and refused to continue.

A few weeks later, he went to Birmingham for a conference. The engineering firm said that to make the trap according to

Sawyer's patented design would be impossibly expensive. After discussion, he agreed to redesign it, and the RSPCA agreed to meet the extra cost. Further trials were held in January 1948, with good results. Sawyer still thought that the traps were too flimsy and would not stand up to hard use, but he thought they would do for the time being and he could make improvements later.

Another meeting to discuss the results took place between the RSPCA, the MAFF, the manufacturers and Sawyer in June 1948. It was agreed to give more strength to the whole assembly, and on this the RSPCA decided that they would mass-produce the trap.

They agreed to have 100,000 manufactured. Sawyer would receive a royalty of 2½d (1p) on each one produced. It was to be known as 'The RSPCA Sawyer Trap'. Sawyer was thus guaranteed a minimum of £1,000, which he badly needed. Much more than the £300 prize had been swallowed up by all the experiments since 1935. Sawyer signed the agreement and was later taken severely to task by Sir Grimwood Mears, who thought – and was almost certainly right – that Sawyer could have obtained much better terms if he had taken the advice of a good solicitor. But Sawyer was no man of business.

So mass-production began and was a disaster. The period of trial had been too short. The traps were still too flimsy; the manufacture was uneven – they differed in strength; many of them were covered with a strong smelling mineral oil, which by its odour was enough to deter rabbits from crossing it. As the traps weathered so the smell of the oil lessened but it also attracted dirt which caused the moving parts to stick. Some improvement was made as production continued but the many complaints caused bitter recriminations between Sawyer, the manufacturers, and the RSPCA. The major part of the blame must fall on the RSPCA, who wasted money given to them in voluntary contributions by going ahead without exhaustive trials. They seem not to have been much better at business than Sawyer – and there was some excuse for him, for he was a river keeper.

In 1951 Sawyer was invited to appear before the Scott Henderson Committee (of the Home Office) on Cruelty to Wild Animals. They recommended that the MAFF should assist in the development of his trap. This they did and a series of really thorough trials began, ending in 1955 with the marketing of the 'Imbra Mark II'. On 1 August 1958 the gin trap became illegal and only traps approved by the MAFF were allowed to be used. Two of these were Sawyer traps.

On this day, when the abolition of the gin was finally achieved, he bought Margaret a bouquet of roses. 'He knew', she said, 'that they would convey to me all that he meant to say, would give me more pleasure than anything else, and would more than compensate for all those lonely hours I spent while he was working on the trap.'

His work was crowned by an award of £1,000 presented to him by Mr W. M. Vane MP, Parliamentary Secretary to the Ministry of Agriculture, Fisheries and Food, at the Ministry on 11 April 1962. By any standards, this was an extraordinary achievement. Sawyer had no engineering training and little education, and the British Government is not noted for its generosity to inventors.

But fate produced a bitterly ironic twist to this long, frustrating story. Myxomatosis arrived and decimated the rabbit population, making the trap superfluous. 'And it was,' said Sawyer, 'a death even more cruel than the gin.'

23

The Sawyer that I Knew

HE CAME UP the bank towards me, picking his way unhurriedly. It was the summer of 1959. I had taken a rod for the season on the SDFFA water, and was curious to meet this river keeper called Sawyer, whose fame had reached the British Army in Germany, from where I had recently returned.

He introduced himself, and we chatted about the river and the fishing prospects for the rest of the day. It was a completely ordinary conversation, such as a river keeper has with his members day in and day out. He was friendly, but correct. He kept his distance and he expected you to keep yours. I remember clearly the impression he made on me. He was a tall, big-boned man, with strong features and deep-set grey eyes. He had a sort of aura of wisdom, which is quite understandable, given that

194

anglers had been coming to him for the past thirty years as to an oracle. For anglers need an oracle. They spend so much of their time totally baffled by the behaviour of the trout, that they turn gratefully to someone like Sawyer, hoping that he will explain the inexplicable. And often he did. Within reason, he enjoyed the role of being the fount of all piscatorial wisdom – who would not? But in his later years it made him somewhat dogmatic. I soon discovered, when I got to know him better, that he did not take kindly to having his opinion – on a fishing matter – questioned.

Something else struck me as unusual about him, and that was the sensitivity in his features. He was a man of Wiltshire, that was apparent. He came of the stock that you can see today in the villages – strong, sturdy men who have worked the land for centuries and lived lives of back-breaking toil. So it is not surprising that this is often reflected in a certain coarseness of feature. But there was nothing coarse about Sawyer's features. They were keen, and his gaze was penetrating. And finally there was his voice: it spoke the broad soft vowels of Wiltshire, but you could sense an intrinsic kindness.

Here was a man, I thought as he went his way, who belonged, who had roots here, who was as much part of this river as the willows and irises, the moorhens and kingfishers, the mayflies and the trout. Later that day, Colonel Evelyn Prendergast (who knew Sawyer well) came up with an amused expression. He had been fishing downstream. 'I met Sawyer earlier,' he said, 'and I asked him if he thought I would get anything if I went to Gunville Hatches. 'All you will get', he replied, 'is tired.'

◊   ◊   ◊

We met from time to time in the sixties without ever being in close or regular contact. These were busy and productive years for him, writing and broadcasting, publishing his theories on chalk, revising *Nymphs and the Trout*, enjoying trips abroad like the one to fish in Bavaria at the invitation of Prince von Quadt, and bringing the Avon fishery to the peak of condition.

His children were marrying and grandchildren were appearing, to add to the joy he had always had in his family life. In 1971, there was a disastrous fire at his home in Court Farm House, Netheravon. A spark caught the thatch and all that could be saved was the contents of his study. His fishing books, rods, and papers were unharmed, but clothes, furniture and household goods were totally destroyed. He and Margaret went to stay with their daughter Pat in the nearby village of Chisenbury. The loss of their comfortable home was a terrible blow. The Army housed them temporarily in a hut on the military airfield at Netheravon, and after eighteen months they moved into the house at Haxton, on the opposite side of the river, where they remained until his death and where Margaret still lives.

◇　　◇　　◇

In 1969, my old friend Brigadier Gilbert Wells, at that time Field Secretary of the Salmon & Trout Association, invited me to become branch organiser for Wiltshire, which I did for the next nine years. Later, my appointment was renamed 'regional chairman', which sounded grander, but I still remained a one-man band. The association at that time went in for grand-sounding names, a natural attempt to cover their basic weakness. They had about 5,000 members out of some three-quarters of a million game fishermen (By 1983, this had increased to 8,200).

I thought it would be useful and enjoyable to run an annual fishing course for children under the aegis of the association. The obvious choice as instructor was Frank Sawyer, and when I asked him he was willing. Together we saw the late Lord Tryon at Great Durnford, on the Avon below Amesbury, and he generously allowed us the use of his lovely stretch of the river, making the stipulation that we should take as many grayling as possible and avoid the trout. Conveniently close was Durnford House School, a preparatory school for girls. In the school holidays, with the kindness of the proprietors, Wing Commander and Mrs Gosse, the school was available for accommodation and catering. As the river teemed with grayling, the set-up seemed ideal.

So it proved. The course became ever more popular, and now a rule has had to be made that a child can attend only once. In the mid-seventies, the Piscatorial Society took over the water and they, with equal generosity, continued the arrangement. For six years, I ran the course with Frank Sawyer and it was during this time that I got to know him well. The serene beauty of that stretch of the Avon, the infectious enthusiasm of the children, and the pleasure of a weekend by the river in his company made it one of my happiest memories.

One never spent time by the river with him without learning something – and not only about how to catch fish. He was not always an easy man to deal with. When we were planning the course, I said: 'Frank, you will not be able to coach twenty children on your own. We can get some help.' I then suggested the names of several well-known fishermen. He glowered at me. 'I don't want any amateurs,' he said. And, as an afterthought, he added, 'If we need help, I will get my son, Tim.' I thought he was being a trifle touchy, but when I knew him better I realised that he had a point. He was a professional, in another league altogether. The only one in his class was, in fact, his son Tim.

A young girl had forgotten her rod and Frank lent her one – a split-cane which had been given him by Charles Ritz. The young lady was soon entangled on the back cast and, heaving at the rod, she broke the top joint irreparably. She managed to keep back the tears until the others gathered round and said – as children will – 'You'll catch it when Mr Sawyer comes!' Then there were floods of tears until Frank came. He comforted her and said that it was not important; and indeed this was true. He would have been happy to fish with a withy stick, as he had done as a boy.

But some things moved him to anger. One was the sight of a fish flapping on the bank and no one making any effort to kill it. 'He has given you your sport,' he would say sternly; 'the least you can do is dispatch him quickly and decently.'

At the end of the two-day course, we used to give the parents a drink by the river when they came to collect their offspring. Social chit-chat did not appeal to Frank, but he endured it, returning polite answers to the oft-repeated question 'How did my Johnny do?' While one of these sessions was in progress, Gilbert Wells arrived. He was the sort of man who Frank liked – full of *joie de vivre*, a fine sportsman, and a true friend – and he had suffered a stroke which had left his right side paralysed. (He taught himself to fish left-handed.) At the sight of him, Frank's habitually severe expression changed. His face lit up, it glowed, there was a warmth and kindliness which was heart-warming to see. It was rare with Frank to see him with his guard down, and it is, sadly, rare in all human contact.

During the drought year, 1976, the course were fishing on Major David Rasch's water a mile or so below Great Durnford.

There was a hatch-pool about seven feet deep and because of the drought there was little flow.

I stood there with Frank's son Tim, who was helping. 'Look,' said Tim, pointing downwards. At the bottom of the pool there was a shoal of at least twenty large grayling. Tim took his rod, with one of Frank's killer bugs on, and lowered it gently into the pool. As the bug descended in front of the noses of the fish, they ignored it completely. Then he lifted the rod, as the bug rose past them one came forward and took it. Tim did it again, and then I did it. When we met for tea, I told Frank the story.

'You say that each time only one came forward?' he asked.

'That's right.'

'You see, they have better manners than human beings.'

It was such incidents that made his company by the river a privilege. That year he suffered without complaint the agonies of an arthritic hip – caused by so much time spent waist-deep in water? – and that winter he had a successful operation for replacement of the hip joint. The next year, 1977, I saw that he had taken to using a stick. At the end, he told me that he felt he could not go on another year. He suggested Mr Douglas Newell of the Wessex Water Authority to replace him. I knew Duggie Newell, and knew that there could be no better choice. But without Frank, it would not be the same. So I handed the course over to Lieutenant-Colonel John Inglis, who had replaced Gilbert Wells as Field Secretary of the Association. They took it on, and it has flourished to this day.

◇   ◇   ◇

What was so special about Frank Sawyer's company by the river? First, of course, his wisdom. The Avon was his river. He knew it as no other human being has ever done, or ever will. If anyone could unfold its mysteries, he could. Then there was the man himself. In his recent book *The River Keeper*, Colonel Richard Pease, who looked after a stretch of the Avon above the SDFFA water, describes Sawyer as 'a man of few words'. How could he write such nonsense, I wondered when I first read it. But on reflection I understood. This was the impression he must have given on first acquaintance to many. Partly, it was the countryman's natural reserve, but it was also a defensive screen which sensitive people often erect to guard their feelings. Not all those he met were true friends like Grimwood Mears or David

Rasch or Ernest Oldrey (for many years Chairman of the SDFFA). Some merely wanted to use his knowledge for their own purposes. Others treated him with thoughtless arrogance. 'Sawyer, go and see if the tea is ready' was the sort of careless remark which hurt him. He took these slights to heart, and put up his guard against them. It often took many years before he decided he could trust you and lowered his guard. But when he did it was immensely rewarding, for there was a natural good-ness and warmth about him. He was utterly without guile. Even in his later years, when one thought he was being dogmatic and refusing to listen to reason, it was impossible to be angry with him, for he spoke with such transparent honesty.

The expression 'compassion for all living creatures' has been used of another great countryman, Thomas Hardy of Dorset – the next county to the west of Wiltshire. It may seem a strange expression to apply to Sawyer, whose job was to provide fish to be killed for sport. Sawyer believed that the fish were put into the rivers by what he called Nature but others would call God to provide sport for man. He saw it as part of the whole scheme of things. Man's part was to tend and nurture. If Man was evil, and damaged his inheritance, then Nature would in the end have her revenge and Man would suffer.

He realised, of course, that there was inescapable cruelty in fishing: but it need not be wanton cruelty. He lived among the wild creatures of the river valley where one kind lived by eating another kind – sometimes by eating its own kind. 'Don't ask me which trout are cannibals,' he told a young child, 'they all are.' One day out shooting with his son Tim, he shot a pheasant – a high, fast bird which had demanded a good shot to bring him down. When they got home, he told Tim to lay the bird on the kitchen table, and they stood in silence before it for a minute to show respect. The bird had given good sport, and had thus fulfilled its purpose.

In the poem 'Afterwards' Thomas Hardy wrote:

> If I pass during some nocturnal blackness, mothy and warm
> When the hedgehog travels furtively over the lawn,
> Will they say 'He strove that such innocent creatures
> should come to no harm'
> But he could do little for them: and now he is gone.

The third line could serve as an epitaph for Frank Sawyer, but not the fourth. He could and did do something for them. In his work for the fishery, he strove to create conditions in which they could thrive. As he wrote, 'I am not one of those who think fishing is all for the human. We should be prepared to share with those who have the greater right.' In the context of this, he was thinking of the otter and the heron – not the pike. Of all creatures, the pike was the only one he hated, because it was an indiscriminate killer. One good-sized pike would take fifty trout in a year and a few would ruin the fishery. He pursued them remorselessly, but even the pike had to be stunned and killed decently.

◇   ◇   ◇

In Sawyer's formative years (the 1920s and 1930s) fishermen argued a good deal about ethics. What was fair and sporting and what was not? In particular, were Skues's nymphs true fly-fishing? It all seems strange today. There is very little in the angling press about ethics. People are obsessed with catching fish, as they are with winning, and the method does not appear to matter. And yet it does matter. Once the novice stage is passed, fishermen discover that some methods are aesthetically satisfying and some are merely boring.

Sawyer was very concerned with ethics. In the 1958 edition of *Nymphs and the Trout* he devoted a chapter to justifying the use of the deep-sunk nymph. In the revised 1970 version he reduced this to a passing reference, for by then his nymphs were generally accepted. He always regarded the dry fly as the highest expression of the art of fly-fishing: the nymph was a supplement, to be used when the dry fly was impossible. Put-and-take was not fishing, but if the rods wanted a harmless bit of fun he had no objection. Hence the construction of the Corfe End lakes at Netheravon in 1964.

There were many modern trends which he did not care for. Whereas before the deep-freeze an angler would stop when he had caught enough for a day or so, now he felt he could go on always for his limit. Whereas, before the pellet, feeding fish in stews was a time-consuming and messy business, now the idle keeper was offered an easy option. The business of stripping gaudy lures through the water he regarded with contempt as just a form of spinning. He deplored the way some fisheries

200

stocked a few huge rainbows and had them caught with full publicity by 'star' anglers. And he reserved his fiercest scorn for those riparian owners who, while pretending to abhor commercialism, in fact exploited the snob appeal of the chalk streams to provide poor fishing and extract every penny they could from the ignorant and credulous angler.

◇ ◇ ◇

Before preparing this book, I had the advantage of knowing Frank Sawyer well. I knew of his compassion, his sensitiveness, his occasional prickliness, his reserve, his humour, and the essential warmth and kindliness. I also thought I was familiar with his work, but in doing the research I have learnt much. I had not realised how big had been his BBC career – more than fifty sound broadcasts and about a dozen television programmes. Nor had I fully appreciated the importance of his work for the river in creating suitable conditions for trout to spawn, and the use of chalk to revive the river. And the story of the humane rabbit trap, which his family think was his finest achievement, would have been a permanent memorial but for the bitter irony of myxomatosis. He was more, much more, than a man who developed a new way of nymph-fishing – though that, in fact, will be his place in history. He will be bracketed with Halford and Skues as one of the giants.

One quality in particular set him apart. Most of us, when we find that something works, are content to leave it at that. A black gnat catches fish, or a pheasant tail nymph does. If they do not, we put it down to the vagaries of the fish. But Sawyer wanted to know why, and he was prepared to study and record and analyse and experiment with utter determination. Thus are the frontiers of knowledge extended.

The word 'genius' is one of those words that is grossly overworked today, and through constant repetition has lost its impact. But if it is defined as the ability to take infinite pains, then Frank Sawyer was a genius.

◇ ◇ ◇

He served the SDFFA for over half a century, and at times they had taken him for granted, but in the later years all was made good. His work was recognised by the award of the MBE in 1978, which gave great pleasure to him and his family. At the Game Fair at Bowood, in north Wiltshire, in 1979, he was awarded the

Country Landowner's Association's long service medal: the cheering when it was presented to him by the Prince of Wales was long and sustained – evidence of his popularity and the affection in which he was held.

By the spring of 1980 he was visibly ageing but he continued his normal life of overseeing the work on the river. After lunch on 18 April, he went out as usual in the car with his dog Shandy. When he had not returned at tea time, Margaret phoned Alan Cook, who had taken over as head keeper. Cook went out to find him, and soon saw his car, parked in the car park adjoining Netheravon church. He noticed that the dog was still in the car, and walked down the path some fifty yards to the river, there known as Choulston shallows, and one of the places Sawyer loved best.

When you walk downstream at this spot, there is first a gently sloping lawn up to an officers' mess, and then the path closes in and becomes quite private. There he came upon Frank Sawyer, lying on his back, his hand still holding his stick, as though asleep. The expression on his face was peaceful. He had been dead for about two hours. It was five o'clock.

After the funeral, he was cremated and his ashes were scattered on the river Avon by the Corfe End lakes at the north end of the village of Netheravon. At the place where this was done they have erected a seat – a plain seat, quite unmarked, just a countryman's seat.

And, nearby, the Avon flows gently on.

Index

203